《中国节庆文化》丛书
编委会名单

顾　问
　　史蒂文·施迈德　　冯骥才　　周明甫
　　黄忠彩　　武翠英　　王国泰

主　编
　　李　松

副主编
　　张　刚　　彭新良

编　委（按姓氏笔画排列）
　　王学文　　田　阡　　邢　莉　　齐勇锋
　　李　旭　　李　松　　杨正文　　杨海周
　　张　刚　　张　勃　　张　跃　　张　暖
　　金　蕾　　赵学玉　　萧　放　　彭新良

List of Members of Editorial Board of *Chinese Festival Culture Series*

Consultants
    Steven Wood Schmader   Feng Jicai   Zhou Mingfu
    Huang Zhongcai   Wu Cuiying   Wang Guotai

Chief Editor
    Li Song

Associate Editor
    Zhang Gang   Peng Xinliang

Members of the Editorial Board

Wang Xuewen	Tian Qian	Xing Li
Qi Yongfeng	Li Xu	Li Song
Yang Zhengwen	Yang Haizhou	Zhang Gang
Zhang Bo	Zhang Yue	Zhang Nuan
Jin Lei	Zhao Xueyu	Xiao Fang
Peng Xinliang		

中国节庆文化丛书
Chinese Festival Culture Series
The Tomb-Sweeping Day

主　编　李　松
副主编　张　刚　彭新良

清明节

田　阡◎著
李　力
石　甜

李建军◎译

全国百佳图书出版单位
时代出版传媒股份有限公司
安徽人民出版社

图书在版编目(CIP)数据

清明节:汉英对照/田阡,石甜著;李力,李建军译.—合肥:安徽人民出版社,2014.1
(中国节庆文化丛书/李松,张刚,彭新良主编)

ISBN 978-7-212-07056-4

Ⅰ.①清… Ⅱ.①田… ②石… ③李… ④李… Ⅲ.①节日—风俗习惯—中国—汉、英 Ⅳ.①K892.1

中国版本图书馆 CIP 数据核字(2013)第 315279 号

Zhongguo Jieqing Wenhua Congshu　Qingmingjie

中国节庆文化丛书　清明节

李　松 **主编** 张　刚　彭新良 **副主编**

田　阡　石　甜 **著** 李　力　李建军 **译**

出 版 人:胡正义　　　　　　　图书策划:胡正义　丁怀超　李　旭
责任编辑:李　莉　陈　蕾　　　装帧设计:宋文岚

出版发行:时代出版传媒股份有限公司 http://www.press-mart.com
　　　　　安徽人民出版社 http://www.ahpeople.com
　　　　　合肥市政务文化新区翡翠路 1118 号出版传媒广场八楼
　　　　　邮编:230071
　　　　　营销部电话:0551—63533258　0551—63533292(传真)
制　　版:合肥市中旭制版有限责任公司
印　　制:安徽新华印刷股份有限公司

开本:710×1010　1/16　　印张:11　　字数:190 千
版次:2014 年 3 月第 1 版　　2014 年 3 月第 1 次印刷

标准书号:ISBN 978-7-212-07056-4　　定价:20.00 元

版权所有,侵权必究

Our Common Days
(Preface)

The most important day for a person in a year is his or her birthday, and the most important days for all of us are the festivals. We can say that the festivals are our common days.

Festivals are commemorating days with various meanings. There are national, ethnic and religious festivals, such as the National Day and Christmas Day, and some festivals for certain groups, such as the Women's Day, the Children's Day and the Labor Day. There are some other festivals closely related to our lives. These festivals have long histories and different customs that have been passed on from one generation to another. There are also different traditional festivals. China is a country full of 56 ethnic groups, and all of the ethnic groups are collectively called the Chinese Nation. Some traditional festivals are common to all people of the Chinese Nation, and some others are unique to certain ethnic groups. For example, the Spring Festival, the Mid-Autumn Day, the Lantern Festival, the Dragon Boat Festival, the Tomb-Sweeping Day and the Double-Ninth Day are common festivals to all of the Chinese people. On the other hand, the New Year of the Qiang Ethnic (a World Cultural Heritage), for example, is a unique festival to the

我们共同的日子
（代序）

个人一年一度最重要的日子是生日，大家一年一度最重要的日子是节日。节日是大家共同的日子。

节日是一种纪念日，内涵多种多样。有民族的、国家的、宗教的，比如国庆节、圣诞节等。有某一类人的，如妇女、儿童、劳动者的，这便是妇女节、儿童节、劳动节等。也有与人们的生活生产密切相关的，这类节日历史悠久，很早就形成了一整套人们约定俗成、代代相传的节日习俗，这是一种传统的节日。传统节日也多种多样。中国是个多民族国家，有五十六个民族，统称中华民族。传统节日有全民族共有的，也有某个民族特有的。比如春节、中秋节、元宵节、端午节、清明节、重阳节等，就为中华民族所

我们共同的日子

共用和共享；世界文化遗产羌年就为羌族独有和独享。各民族这样的节日很多。

传统节日是在漫长的农耕时代形成的。农耕时代生产与生活、人与自然的关系十分密切。人们或为了感恩于大自然的恩赐，或为了庆祝辛苦劳作换来的收获，或为了激发生命的活力，或为了加强人际的亲情，经过长期相互认同，最终约定俗成，渐渐把一年中某一天确定为节日，并创造了十分完整又严格的节俗，如仪式、庆典、规制、禁忌，乃至特定的游艺、装饰与食品，来把节日这天演化成一个独具内涵和迷人的日子。更重要的是，人们在每一个传统的节日里，还把共同的生活理想、人间愿望与审美追求融入节日的内涵与种种仪式中。因此，它是中华民族世间理想与生活愿望极致的表现。可以说，我们的传统——精神文化传统，往往就是依靠这代代相传的一年一度的节日继承下来的。

Qiang Ethnic Group, and there are many festivals celebrated only by minorities in China.

The traditional festivals are formed throughout the long agrarian age, during which the relationships between life and production and between the people and the nature were very close. To express the gratitude to the nature for its gifts, or celebrate the harvests from hard works, or stimulate the vitality of life, or strengthen the relationships among people, people would determine one day in a year as a festival with complete and strict customs, such as ceremonies, rules and taboos, special activities, decorations and foods to make the festival a day with unique meanings and charms. More importantly, people would integrate their good wishes into the meanings and ceremonies of the festivals. Therefore, the festivals could represent the ideals and wishes of the people in the best way. It is safe to say that our traditions, more specifically, our spiritual and cultural traditions, are inherited through the festivals year by year.

Our Common Days

However, since the 20th century, with the transition from the agricultural civilization to the industrial civilization, the cultural traditions formed during the agrarian age have begun to collapse. Especially in China, during the process of opening up in the past 100 years, the festival culture, especially the festival culture in cities, has been impacted by the modern civilization and foreign cultures. At present, the Chinese people have felt that the traditional festivals are leaving away day by day so that some worries are produced about this. With the diminishing of the traditional festivals, the traditional spirits carried by them will also disappear. However, we are not just watching them disappearing, but actively dealing with them, which could fully represent the self-consciousness of the Chinese people in terms of culture.

In those ten years, with the fully launching of the folk culture heritage rescue program of China, and the promotion of the application for national non-material cultural heritage list, more attention has been paid to the traditional festivals, some of which have been added to the central cultural heritage list. After that, in 2006, China has determined that the second Saturday of June of each year shall be the Cultural Heritage Day, and in 2007, the State Council added three important festivals, namely the Tomb-sweeping Day, the Dragon Boat Festival and the Mid-Autumn Day, as the legal holidays. These decisions have showed that our government

然而，自从二十世纪整个人类进入了由农耕文明向工业文明的过渡，农耕时代形成的文化传统开始瓦解。尤其是中国，在近百年由封闭走向开放的过程中，节日文化——特别是城市的节日文化受到现代文明与外来文化的冲击。当下人们已经鲜明地感受到传统节日渐行渐远，并为此产生忧虑。传统节日的淡化必然使其中蕴含的传统精神随之涣散。然而，人们并没有坐等传统的消失，主动和积极地与之应对。这充分显示了当代中国人在文化上的自觉。

近十年，随着中国民间文化遗产抢救工程的全面展开，国家非物质文化遗产名录申报工作的有力推动，传统节日受到关注，一些重要的传统节日列入了国家文化遗产名录。继而，2006年国家将每年六月的第二个周六确定为"文化遗产日"；2007年国务院决定将三个中华民族的重要节日——清明节、端午节和中秋节

我们共同的日子

列为法定放假日。这一重大决定，表现了国家对公众的传统文化生活及其传承的重视与尊重，同时也是保护节日文化遗产十分必要的措施。

节日不放假必然直接消解了节日文化，放假则是恢复节日传统的首要条件。但放假不等于远去的节日立即就会回到身边。节日与假日的不同是因为节日有特定的文化内容与文化形式。那么，重温与恢复已经变得陌生的传统节日习俗则是必不可少的了。

千百年来，我们的祖先从生活的愿望出发，为每一个节日都创造出许许多多美丽又动人的习俗。这种愿望是理想主义的，所以节日习俗是理想的；愿望是情感化的，所以节日习俗也是情感化的；愿望是美好的，所以节日习俗是美的。人们用合家团聚的年夜饭迎接新年；把天上的明月化为手中甜甜的月饼，来象征人间的团圆；在严寒刚刚消退、万物复苏的早春，赶到野外去打扫墓地，告慰亡灵，

emphasizes and respects the traditional cultural activities and their heritages. Meanwhile, these are important measures to protect festival cultural heritages.

Festivals without holidays will directly harm the festival culture. Holiday is the most important condition for the recovery of a festival, but holiday does not mean that the festival will come back immediately. Festivals are different from holidays because festivals have unique cultural contents and forms. Therefore, it will be necessary to review and recover the customs of the traditional festivals that have become strange to us.

For thousands of years, our ancestors created beautiful and moving customs for each festival based on their best wishes. The customs are ideal, since the wishes are ideal. The customs are emotional, since the wishes are emotional. The customs are beautiful, since the wishes are beautiful. We have the family reunion dinner to receive a new year. We make moon cakes according to the shape of the moon in the mid-autumn to symbolize the reunion of our family. We visit the tombs of our ancestors in the early spring and go outing to beautiful and green hills to express our grief. These beautiful festival customs have offered us great comfort and peace for generations.

Our Common Days

To ethnic minorities, their unique festivals are of more importance, since these festivals bear their common memories and represent their spirits, characters and identities.

Who ever can say that the traditional customs are out of date? If we have forgotten these customs, we should review them. The review is not imitating the customs of our ancients, but experiencing the spirits and emotions of the traditions with our heart.

During the course of history, customs are changing, but the essence of the national tradition will not change. The tradition is to constantly pursue a better life, to be thankful to the nature and to express our best wishes for family reunion and the peace of the world.

This is the theme of our festivals, and the reason and purpose of this series of books.

The planning and compiling of the series is unique. All of the festivals are held once a year. Since China is a traditional agricultural society,

表达心中的缅怀，同时戴花插柳，踏青春游，亲切地拥抱大地山川……这些诗意化的节日习俗，使我们一代代人的心灵获得了美好的安慰与宁静。

对于少数民族来说，他们特有的节日的意义则更加重要。节日还是他们民族集体记忆的载体、共同精神的依托、个性的表现、民族身份之所在。

谁说传统的习俗过时了？如果我们淡忘了这些习俗，就一定要去重温一下传统。重温不是表象地模仿古人的形式，而是用心去体验传统中的精神与情感。

在历史的进程中，习俗是在不断变化的，但民族传统的精神本质不应变。这传统就是对美好生活不懈的追求，对大自然的感恩与敬畏，对家庭团圆与世间和谐永恒的企望。

这便是我们节日的主题，也是这套节庆丛书编写的根由与目的。

这套书的筹划独具匠心。所有节日都是一年一次。由于我国为传统农

我们共同的日子

耕社会，所以生活与生产同步，节日与大自然的节气密切相关。本丛书以一年的春、夏、秋、冬四个时间板块，将纷繁的传统节日清晰有序地排列开来，又总揽成书，既包括全民族共有的节日盛典，也把少数民族重要的节日遗产纳入其中，以周详的文献和生动的传说，将每个节日的源起、流布与习俗，亦图亦文、有滋有味地娓娓道来。一节一册，单用方便，放在一起则是中华民族传统节日的一部全书，既有知识性、资料性、工具性，又有阅读性和趣味性。这样一套丛书不仅是对我国传统节日的一次总结，也是对传统节日文化富于创意的弘扬。

我读了书稿，心生欣喜，因序之。

冯骥才
2013.12.25

the life is synchronized with production, and the festivals are closely relevant to the climates. In this series, all of the traditional festivals in China will be introduced in the order of the four seasons, covering the common festivals as well as important ethnic festivals that have been listed as cultural heritages. All of the festivals are described in detail with texts and images to introduce their origins, customs and distribution. Each book of the series is used to introduce one festival so that it is convenient to read individually and it may be regarded as a complete encyclopedia if connected with each other. Therefore, it is not only intellectual, informative and instrumental, but also readable and interesting. The series could be used as a tool book or read for leisure. It is not only the summary of the traditional festivals of our country, but an innovative promotion of our traditional festival culture.

I felt very delighted after reading the manuscript, so I wrote this preface.

Feng Jicai
December 25th, 2013

目 录 / Contents

第一章 起源
Chapter One Origin

1 上巳节
The Shangsi Festival /003

2 寒食节
The Hanshi Festival /015

3 祭祖
Ancestor Worship /025

4 节气
Solar Nodes or Terms /034

5 清明节
The Qingming Festival /041

第二章 流布
Chapter Two Dissemination

1 大陆
Mainland China /047

2 港台
Hong Kong and Taiwan /078

3 海外
Overseas Chinese Communities /081

目 录
Chapter Three Customs 第三章 风俗

1. 扫墓与祭祖
   Tomb Sweeping and Ancestor Worshipping /091
2. 踏青
   Go for an Outing in Early Spring /096
3. 饮食
   Food /109

第四章 特色节庆地
Chapter Four Distinctive Festive Places

1. 陕西：清明公祭
   Shaanxi Province: Qingming Public Memorial /135
2. 少数民族过清明
   National Minorities Celebrate Qingming /137
3. 苏北水乡：清明大会船
   Waterland in Northern Jiangsu Province: Regatta /141

后 记
Postscript /160

《中国节庆文化》丛书后记
The Postscript of *Chinese Festival Culture Series* /163

第一章 起源

"清明时节雨纷纷,路上行人欲断魂。借问酒家何处有,牧童遥指杏花村。"唐代大诗人杜牧的一首《清明》,流传至今。作为中华民族的传统节日,清明节期间扫墓祭祖的习俗一直被人民群众所继承。但是,扫墓祭祖并不是从来就有的,而清明节的活动也不只是这两项。事实上,现在的清明节是融合了古代的上巳节、寒食节和春祭,在历史的长河中慢慢演变而来的传统节日。

Chapter One
Origin

"A drizzling rain falls ceaselessly on the Mourning Day;
The mourner's heart is breaking on his way.
'Where can I find a tavern, please?'
'Over there.' A cowherd points to Almond Flower Village in the distance."

This is a poem entitled *Qingming* by the great Tang Dynasty poet Du Mu, which is still popular today. As a traditional Chinese festival, the practice of sweeping the ancestral tombs and honoring their ancestors during the Qingming Festival has been inherited by the Chinese people. However, tending to the graves of the departed ones or offering sacrifices to the ancestors didn't exist at all times, nor were the Qingming activities just limited to these two, either. In fact, the present-day Qingming Festival is the integration of the ancient Shangsi Festival, Hanshi Festival and spring offerings and has evolved gradually into a traditional festival in the long process of history.

Chapter One
Origin

1 上巳节
The Shangsi Festival

The Shangsi Festival refers to the first Si day in March, that is, the third day of the third month of the Chinese calendar. The emergence of this festival was originally related with Taoism. In the Chinese folk tales and legends, Xiwangmu (the Queen Mother of the West) is a fairy living in mythical Kunlun Mountains of the West, who has three ferocious birds named Qingniao (Blue or Green Bird) serving her. According to the records of *Zhen Zhong Shu,* or *Book in a Pillow* by Ge Hong, a minor southern official during the Jin Dynasty of China, at a time of pre-Creation when the Universe was still null and the cosmos was in disorder, the Spirit of Heaven and Earth, called Yuanshi Tianwang, literally "Heavenly King of the Primordial Beginning" was roaming in the midst of where Heaven and Earth were once inextricably commingled (hun-dun). Later, Liangyi, or *Yin* and *Yang*, were produced. Yuanshi Tianwang, residing above the center of Heaven, inhaled Heavenly air, drank Earthly springs. After being

上巳，指农历三月第一个巳日。上巳节的出现，最初与道教有关。在中国民间传说中，西王母是住在西方昆仑山的仙女，有三只名为"青鸟"的猛禽伺候她。晋朝葛洪的《枕中书》记载，混沌未开之前，号称"元始天王"的天地之精游走于混沌之中，后来二仪化分，元始天王居天中心之上，吸天气，饮地泉，又经数劫，与太元玉女通气结精，生天皇西王母。因而，每年三月初三是西王母的生日。王母娘娘的蟠桃园里有三千六百株蟠桃树，她每年生日的时候都会举办蟠桃会，而瑶池蟠

第一章 起源

桃会又引出了"麻姑献寿"的故事。

麻姑是南北朝时期的一位北方少数民族姑娘。她自幼失去母亲，与父亲相依为命。她从小就学了一手好针线活，为有钱人家做活。有一天，主人赏给了她一个大桃子，麻姑舍不得吃，想带回家给父亲。在回家的路上，她看见路边围了一群人，走过去一看，发现地上躺了一位身着黄衫的老婆婆，奄奄一息。有人说，老婆婆饿坏了，如果吃点东西，就好了。麻姑拿出桃子给老婆婆吃，老婆婆很快就醒来，对麻姑说："孩子，你可不可以再给我喂点粥汤？"麻姑答应了，她把老婆婆扶到街边的屋檐下坐着，之后回家生

through suffering Karma, Yuanshi Tianwang mated with Taiyuan Yünü (the Virgin of the Great Origin) and produced Tianhuang (the God of Heaven) and Xiwangmu, the possessor of the garden of the 3600 sacred peach trees. March the third is the birthday of Xiwangmu. Xiwangmu would celebrate her birthday, the third day of the third lunar month , by hosting a Pantao (Chinese flat peach-immortality peach) banquet at the Pond of Jade each year. And the assembly also brought about the story of Ma Gu, who presented her birthday gift to Xiwangmu.

Ma Gu was a northern ethnic minority girl during the Southern and Northern Dynasties. She lost her mother when she was very young and lived with her father ever since. She was very good at needle work and served as a maid for the rich families. One day, her mistress gave her a peach as a reward. Instead of eating it all by herself, she wanted to take it home to her father. On her way back home, she saw a crowd of people along the roadside. She went over and found an old woman in yellow lying there dying. Some said that the old woman was starving to death and that she would be all right if she ate something. Ma Gu took the peach out to feed the old woman. Then the woman awoke immediately and asked if she could kindly feed her some porridge. Ma Gu said yes. She helped the old woman sit under the roof on the street for a rest and went back home, lighting the fire to cook the porridge. When Ma Gu's father came back home, he got to know what happened. It turned out that he wouldn't allow his daughter to bring the porridge to the old woman nor

Chapter One
Origin

let her out.

At midnight, Ma Gu sneaked out. She looked for the old woman everywhere but only found a peach pit under the roof. She picked it up and brought it back home. The next night, Ma Gu dreamed of the old woman in yellow who said to her, "Thank you, my dear. That peach is very tasty. I will live long enough after eating it. Please rest assured." Ma Gu woke up and planted the peach pit in her own yard. One year later, a big peach tree grew out. In the first month of the lunar calendar every year, the peach tree would be blooming and bear a lot of big and red peaches in lunar March. Ma Gu gave the peaches to the poor old people. After eating the peaches, not only would they not feel hungry without eating for days, they were also recovered from diseases. Everybody said that Ma Gu is an immortal from Heaven. In every lunar March, she would present peaches, which was called Ma Gu Xian Shou, literally Ma Gu Offers Longevity. Ma Gu didn't know until then that the old woman in yellow was Lishan Laomu or Mother Goddess of Mt. Li, the revered Taoist goddess in ancient times who guided Ma Gu to cultivate herself and become an immortal. From then on, Ma Gu would distribute peaches among poor old people in every lunar March.

In addition, based on the ancient legends, Nüwa handcrafted seven animals in seven days which were

火煮粥。麻姑的父亲回家后，听说了这件事情，既不许麻姑给老婆婆送粥，也不许她外出。

半夜，麻姑偷偷溜出去找老婆婆，却见屋檐下只有一颗桃核在那里，就捡起来带回家。第二天晚上，麻姑梦见黄衫老婆婆对她说：“孩子，谢谢你，那桃子很好，我吃了已经足够益寿延年了，你放心吧。”麻姑醒来，把桃核种在自家院子里，一年之后就长成一棵大桃树。这棵桃树每年正月里开花，三月里就结出又大又红的桃子。麻姑将桃子送给穷困的老人们，老人们吃了麻姑送的桃子之后，不仅几天不吃饭都不觉得饿，而且原来的病也都好了。大家都说麻姑是天仙下凡，每年三月送桃时就称之为"麻姑献寿"。后来麻姑才知道，那位黄衫老婆婆是道教远古尊神骊山老母，她带麻姑去修道成仙了。从此以后，每年三月，麻姑还是经常送桃给贫困的老人们。

此外，根据古代传说，女娲娘娘在七天之内

第一章 起源

捏制出七种动物，并且分别给它们安排了日期，初一是鸡日、初二是狗日、初三为羊日、初四为猪日、初五为牛日、初六是马日、初七为人日。但是，按照天干地支的排序法，初七又是地支巳日，所以巳日即人日。巳对应的生肖和神兽是蛇，蛇象征着生殖和生命。在人日这一天，人们制作"七宝羹"和"薰天"两种食物。七宝羹是用七种菜做的菜肴，薰天是露天做的煎饼。此外，还要用五彩丝品剪成人形或用金箔刻成人形挂在屏风或帐子上，以保平安。

早在先秦时期就已经有对上巳节的庆祝了。郑国以三月上旬的巳日为其祭高禖、大会男女的节日。人们在野外或水边召唤亲人亡魂，《诗经·郑风·溱洧》曰："谓今三月桃花水下，以招魂续魄，祓除岁秽……三月上巳之辰，此两水之上招魂续魄，拂除不祥。"当时，郑国的风俗是要在这一天，去水边"招魂

respectively designated as the days of the rooster, dog, sheep, pig, cow, horse and man. However, based on the sequential method of the Tiangan Dizhi, or Ten Heavenly Stems and Twelve Earthly Branches, the seventh day is also the Si Day of the Earthly Branches, so Si Day is called Man's Day. The corresponding Chinese Zodiac animal is snake, a symbol of reproduction and life. On Man's Day, people would make two kinds of foods. One is called Qibao Geng, a dish made of seven vegetables; the other is Xun Tian, a kind of pancake made outdoors. Apart from this, figures were cut or carved out of five-colored silk or gold foil to be hung on the screens or bed curtains for the purpose of peace and safety.

As early as the Pre-Qin Period, the remote antiquity before Emperor Qinshihuang united China for the first time in 221 B.C., the Shangsi Festival

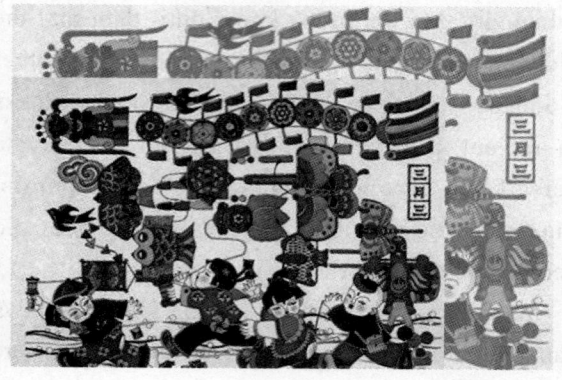

Chapter One
Origin

was already celebrated. In the State of Zheng, the Si Day in early March was the festival for offering sacrifices to the Goddess of Marriage and Women's Fertility and dating. During the festival, people would outside or waterside to call back the spirits of the deceased beloved. The classic of poetry reads, "On the waters near the peach on March 3rd, rituals were held to call back the spirit of the dead, get rid of the annual filth and ward off evil spirits". At that time, the practice in the State of Zheng was that on that day people would go to the riverside to call back the spirits and get them back. To those revering ghosts and spirits, it is very unlucky for ghosts and spirits to return to the human world. That is why the people in the State of Zheng considered the lunar March unlucky and would bathe to ward off evils and diseases, which later developed into the ceremonial service of bathing in the water to get rid of bad luck and illnesses. *The Analects of Confucius* says, "In late spring, when spring clothes were ready, there would be five or six hatted young men and six or seven kids who would bathe in the Yi River and dance in the wind and sing all the way back home afterwards." And "bathe in the Yi River in later spring" refers to the rituals that officials and common people bathed in the herbal water outside to get rid of the filth from their bodies, drive away diseases and evils and keep off bad luck during the Shangsi Festival. *Luoxi Fu* by Zhang Xie, the Jin Dynasty writer, reads, "I'd like to sing an ode to the second month of spring-enshrouding mists, a gentle breeze and blooming fragrant flowers are a riot

续魄"，把鬼魂找回来。对于敬畏神灵鬼魂的人而言，鬼魂回到人间的话，是相当不吉利的，所以郑国人同时也认为"三月不祥"，需要用沐浴等方式赶走邪气，于是就有了后来的"祓禊洗澡"的习俗。《论语·先进·侍坐章》云："暮春者，春服既成，冠者五六人，童子六七人，浴乎沂，风乎舞雩，咏而归。"而"暮春浴乎沂"即三月上巳祓禊洗澡之浴，人们用浸泡了香草的水沐浴，驱散疾病和不祥的仪式。三月"上巳，官民皆絜于东流水尚，曰洗濯祓除，去宿垢疢，为大絜"。祓禊也就是在郊外水滨进行沐浴，以达到洗除污垢、除灾去凶的目的。晋张协《洛禊赋》曰："夫何三春之令月，嘉天气之氤氲，和风穆以布畅兮，百卉晔而敷芳。川流清泠以汪秽，原隰葱翠以龙鳞。"

第一章 起源

除了祓禊沐浴之外，还有在河边"解神"的活动，即还愿谢神。汉代王充在《论衡》中说："世间善治宅舍，凿地掘土，功成作解谢土神，名曰谢神。"束晳答晋武帝曲水之问提到的"周公卜筮定东都，建成后流水泛杯而饮"的故事，也是一种得福于天的欢欣与酬谢；北朝周人庾信还有《春赋》："三日曲水向河津，日晚河边多解神。树下流杯客。沙头渡水人。"此外，在上巳节期间，也有用明火来驱除不祥的，并且一直保留在民俗中。如山东齐河县视三月三为神节，小孩子是天上的童子投胎转世，在三月三这一天会被召回去，所以为了防止小孩夭折，家家户户请巫师扎彩纸人，用火焚烧，以欺骗上天误以为已经把童子召回去了，这个仪式叫作"换身"。

of colors. Rivers are overflowing with crystal and cold water. The dragon scale–like fields are a lush verdancy."

In addition to the sacrificial bathing ceremony, there was an activity at the riverside called Jieshen, a ceremony to thank god for the promise fulfillment. Wang Chong of the Han Dynasty said in his *Lunheng*, or *Critical Essays*, "People who are good at managing houses would dig earth and thank the God of Land, called Xieshen (thank god)". The Western Jin litterateur Shu Xi, in reply to the question put forward by Emperor Wu of Jin about the Qu River, once mentioned the story that the Duke of Zhou Dynasty decided to make Luoyang the capital by divination and drank wine from the cups floating on the water afterwards, which is also a kind of joy from Heaven and gratitude to god. *Chun Fu* by Yu Xin, a Northern Zhou Dynasty poet also reads, "On March 3rd, towards the ferry the river winds its way; along the river at dusk, to gods many people redeem their vows and prayers. Under the trees gather cup-floating drinkers, by the sandbank wait travelers." In addition, during the Shangsi Festival, open fire was also used to ward off unluckiness, which has been kept in the folk customs. For example, the March 3rd was regarded as the Festival of Gods in Qihe county, Shangdong Province. Little kids on Earth are reincarnated from deities in Heaven who would be called back on the third day of the third month. Therefore, in order to prevent little kids from dying, every household would ask sorcerers to make colorful paper figures

Chapter One
Origin

and burn them to make such an illusion that the Heavenly deities have been already called back. This ceremony is called "Body Exchange".

During the Qin and Han Dynasties, the customs of the Shangsi Festival in the third month remained. And during the Shangsi Festival of the Han Dynasty, the main concern was infertility. Young people woukd indulge themselves near the riverside for the purpose of reproduction, as recorded in *Nandu Fu*, or *Southern Capital Rhapsody* by Zhang Heng, "On the day of Shangsi in late spring, the cleaning ceremony takes place at the northern bank of the river where countless carriages gather to pray to gods for blessings." *Han Shu*: *Ben Ji*, or *The Book of the [Former] Han Dynasty*: *Imperial Biographies* reads, "After ascending to the throne for several years, Emperor Wu of Han, was not able to bear a single son. So Princess Ping Yang bought 10 maidens and had them dressed up to wait for the emperor. On Shangsi Festival, the emperor paid her a visit." One of the pray-for-sons activities during the Shangsi Festival was to put such symbolic objects as floating eggs, floating dates and floating plums in the water.

During the Han Dynasty, the custom of going on an outing for entertainment came into being. Based on *Xijing Zaji*, "Emperor Gaozu of Han and Consort Qi, his favorite concubine would go on an outing on March 3rd and climb the mountains on Sept. 9th". About the origin of the Shangsi Festival, based on the folk tales during the Wei and Jin Dynasties, Zhou Chu of the Jin Dynasty in his *Fengtu Ji* said,

秦汉时期，三月上巳节日的习俗继承下来，汉代的上巳节，所针对的疾病主要是不育，人们在水边放纵，以求生育，即是张衡在《南都赋》里所记录的"暮春之禊，元巳之辰，方轨齐轸，祓于阳濒"。《汉书·本纪》云："武帝即位，数年无子，平阳公主求良家女十余人，饰置其家。帝上巳祓禊灞上而过焉。"上巳求子行事之一，是在水中放入浮卵、浮枣、浮李的象征物。

汉代时逐渐有了游乐之俗。《西京杂记》云："汉高祖与戚夫人三月上巳，九月重阳，士女游春，就北祓禊登高。"上巳节的来历来自于魏晋民间传说。晋代周处的《风土记》载："汉末离

第一章 起源

开虞者有三女，一以三月上辰，一以上巳，一以上午，三日三女乳时并亡。迄今时俗以为大忌，故至是月是日，妇人忌讳不复止家，皆适东流水上就通远地，祈祓自洁濯也。"根据东汉郑玄的解释，上巳与登假（遐）可相转训，则上巳又有死亡、升天之意。

"At the end of the Han Dynasty, there were three girls who left the State of Yu (in present-day Shanxi Province) on the days of the first *Chen, Si* and *Wu* of the third lunar month respectively (based on the 'heavenly stem-earthly branch recording method' in ancient China). Unfortunately, all of them died when they gave birth to a child. Thus today the three days are customarily regarded as a big taboo during which women would no longer stay at home but go to the riverside leading to boundaries far away to bathe in order to clean themselves to ward off evils". According to the explanation of Zheng Xuan, the famous Eastern Han Dynasty Confucian scholar, Shangsi has the connotation of death and going up to Heaven.

Chapter One
Origin

And an anecdote called Qushui Liushang, literally glasses of wine floating on the Qushui River, also evolved from the Shangsi Festival. During Wei and Jin Dynasties, officials would hold the ceremony of bathing to get rid of filth and diseases. At the same time, the entertainment feast along the riverside were added accompanied by chanting poems while drinking from the drifting cups along the winding river. This activity was recorded as Qushui Liushang, literally "liquor cups floating on the winding brook, a game played in ancient China, in *Lanting Jixu*, or *Preface to the Poems Composed at the Orchid Pavilion* by Wang Xizhi. On March 3rd of the ninth year of the Yonghe Era during the reign of the Emperor Mu of Jin Dynasty, the well-known calligrapher Wang Xizhi, invited 41 friends and relatives including Xie An, a Jin Dynasty statesman and Sun Chuo, a Chinese poet of the Six Dynasties poetry tradition, to join him at the Orchid Pavilion surrounded by towering peaks and verdant undergrowth for the purification rites of spring, sharing cups of liquor and allowing the full cups to drift downstream. This practice has continued until today. At that time, after the purification ceremony, Wang Xizhi sat with other scholars and poets by the Orchid Pavilion, chanting poems while drinking from the drifting cups along the winding river. If the cups swirled and stopped in front of whoever of the group before escaping to the wider river, that person was supposed to spontaneously create a poem and knock back the cup. Based on the historical record, at this gathering, there were 11 people who

由上巳节还演化出一段"曲水流觞"的逸事。魏晋时，士大夫在祓禊的同时，还要举行水滨宴会，谈文作赋，饮酒取乐。饮酒时，要将酒杯置于流水之中，酒杯随水流动，到谁的面前，谁就要饮酒吟诗。这个活动，在著名书法家、文学家王羲之的《兰亭集序》中被记为"曲水流觞"。永和九年（353年）三月初三上巳日，晋代有名的大书法家、会稽内史王羲之偕亲朋谢安、孙绰等四十二人，在兰亭修禊后，举行饮酒赋诗的"曲水流觞"活动，引为千古佳话。这一儒风雅俗，一直流传至今。当时，王羲之等在举行修禊祭祀仪式后，在兰亭清溪两旁席地而坐，将盛了酒的觞放在溪中，由上游浮水徐徐而下，经过弯弯曲曲的溪流，觞在谁的面前打转或停下，谁就即兴赋诗并饮酒。据史载，在这次游戏中，有十一人各成诗两篇，十五人各成诗一篇，十六人作不出诗，各罚酒三觥。

第一章 起源

王羲之将大家的诗集起来，在蚕茧纸上用鼠须笔挥毫作序，乘兴而书，写下了举世闻名的《兰亭集序》，被后人誉为"天下第一行书"，王羲之也因之被人尊为"书圣"。

此后，上巳节逐渐与寒食节、清明节等融合在一起，人们不再单独庆祝上巳节，但其节庆活动，包括曲水流觞、踏青沐浴等内容，依然流传下来。唐朝时，三月三日上巳节被禊色彩日趋淡化，增加了水边游乐的成分。宋代上巳节时，还有感应乞子石以求子的习俗。唐宋时此俗尚盛行。

清代仍然有三月三出游的习俗。河南泌阳县"人多出游，追上巳拔除之遗风"；江西瑞州府"携酒盒郊游踏青，士民皆然"；安徽歙县古意较浓，"竞渡龙舟于河或况

produced 2 poems respectively, 15 people who composed 1 poem respectively and 16 people who wrote none and were urged to drink 3 cups of wine as a punishment. The poems were collected, and Wang Xizhi himself wrote *the Preface to the Orchid Pavilion Collection* in Xingshu, a semi-cursive script. It is among the most well-known and most-copied pieces of calligraphy in Chinese history, called No.1 cursive handwriting in the country, and Wang Xizhi was therefore acclaimed as the Sage of Calligraphy.

Later, the Shangsi Festival was gradually mingled together with the Hanshi Festival and Qingming Festival. People stopped celebrating the Shangsi Festival specifically. However, the festive activities including Qushui Liushang, spring outings, as well as taking a bath to get rid of filth and so on, still spread down. During the Tang Dynasty, the religious ceremony of eliminating disasters and begging for blessings on the Double-Third Festival gradually faded away and developed into an outing by the water. During the Song Dynasty, there was also a practice to pray and beg the Qizi (beg-son) stone for sons. This custom was very popular in the Tang-Song period.

During the Qing Dynasty, there still existed a custom of going sight-seeing on the third day of the third month. In Miyang County, Henan Province, "most of the people would follow the Shangsi custom and go out for a trip for the purpose of getting rid of filth and diseases". In Ruizhou, Jiangxi Province, all the people, "officials and

Chapter One
Origin

civilians alike, would go outside carrying wine boxes and enjoy the greenery of springtime". And in Shexian County, Anhui Province, "the local people would even hold Dragon Boat Races in water or build land boats, called Fuzhu, a religious activity of eliminating disasters and begging for blessings". Apart from outings, there was an activity of dispelling vermin on the third day of the third lunar month during the Qing Dynasty. In some places of Northern China, willow branches would be plucked to ward off scorpions. For example, in Wuxiang County, Shanxi Province, "ten people would insert willow branches into walls to drive away poisonous scorpions". And in the South, it was customary to dispel insects and ants. *Qing Jia Lu* says, a popular saying in Suzhou, Jiangsu Province goes "Ants get together on the top of kitchen range on the third day of the third lunar month." So on that day every family would put wild flowers on the kitchen range to dispel insects and ants. The wild flowers used in Suzhou to dispel insects and

渡河干，或造舟陆游，存修禊意，又名祓祝"。除了出游，清代的臣民过三月三，还有抑制害虫的活动。北方的一些地区是折柳避蝎，山西武乡县"十人取柳枝遍插墙壁间，谓之驱毒蝎"。南方则有驱除虫蚁的风俗。《清嘉录》说苏州"因谚有'三月三，蚂蚁上灶山'之语，三日人家皆以野菜花置灶台上，以厌虫蚁"。苏州"厌虫蚁"用的野菜花，实际是荠菜花。苏州妇女还有戴荠菜花的习惯，"妇女簪髻上，以祈清目，俗号眼亮花"。河南新蔡县与此不同，"戴荠花，盖以丰年甘草先生，故戴之，喜岁十也"。福建永福县"采香草插门，以祓不祥"。清代三月三日还有祀真武神的活动。总之，清代三月三日有郊游踏青、戴荠插柳、抑制蚁蝎、祭祀神灵的风俗。

第一章 起源

ants were actually shepherd's purse flowers. Suzhou women also have the habit of wearing shepherd's purse flowers on the head, "women would put on shepherd's purse flowers on the head to pray for having bright eyes, and therefore shepherd's purse flowers are also called eye-clearing flowers". On the contrary, in Xincai County, Henan Province, women would "wear shepherd's purse flowers on the head in a good year for the good of their husbands". And in Yongfu County, Fujian Province, "fragrant grass would be put on the doors to get rid of evils". In addition, during the Qing Dynasty, on March 3rd, the ceremony of worshipping the martial god was also held. In conclusion, on the third day of the third lunar month during the Qing Dynasty, there were various customs and practices such as going out for a walk, wearing shepherd's purse flowers on the head, inserting willow branches on gates, ridding of ants and scorpions, and offering sacrifices to gods and spirits as well.

Chapter One
Origin

2 寒食节
The Hanshi Festival

The Hanshi Festival, or the Cold Food Festival, originated from a sad and miserable story. Based on *Lüshi Chunqiu*, or *Mister Lü's Spring and Autumn Annals*, Jie Zitui, a native of the State of Jin during the Spring and Autumn Period was a faithful follower to Chong'er, Duke Wen of Jin. After 19 years of exile, Duke Wen granted titles to his meritorious followers. To Duke Wen's surprise, Jie Zitui was not the type of person who sought rewards but declined his invitation instead. Jie Zitui's neighbor felt so unfair that he wrote a letter at night and hung it at the city gate. Duke Wen of Jin didn't know that Jie Zitui was living in seclusion in Mount Mian, Shanxi Province, until after reading the letter and sent for Jie Zitui to be conferred.

Duke Wen of Jin himself brought his men to Mount Mian to look for Jie Zitui for several days in succession but in vain. Being extremely earnest

寒食节来自于一个悲伤又凄惨的故事。据《吕氏春秋》记载，介子推（又名介之推）是春秋时期晋国人，是晋文公重耳手下的忠臣。重耳结束十九年逃亡生活后，分封贤臣。介子推认为身为臣下，忠诚是理所当然的事情，因而不肯受赏。邻居替他打抱不平，夜里写了封书信挂到城门上。晋文公看到此信后，派人召介子推受封，才知道他已隐入绵山。

晋文公亲自带领人马前往绵山，寻访几日都没有见到介子推的身

第一章 起源

影。晋文公求人心切，下令烧山，试图逼迫介子推现身。没料到大火烧了三天，连介子推的影子也没见到。后来有人在一棵枯柳树下发现了介子推和他母亲的尸骨，晋文公悲痛万分，将一段烧焦的柳木带回宫中做了一双木屐，每天望着它叹道："悲哉足下。"晋文公命人将介子推葬于绵山，并改绵山为介山，下令之推焚死之日禁火寒食，以寄哀思。

"子推言避世，山火遂焚身。四海同寒食，千秋为一人。"唐代诗人卢象这首《寒食》诗，表达了后人纪念介子推的崇敬之意。虽然寒食节逐渐得到推广，但是并不是所有人都赞同冷食禁火的习俗。记载了汉代寒食节习俗的范晔《后汉书·周举传》云：

周举迁并州刺史，太原一郡，旧俗以介之推焚骸，有龙忌之禁，至其月咸言神灵不乐举火，移书于之推庙云："春中寒食一月，老小不堪，今则三

to find Jie Zitui, Duke Wen ordered his men to set the Mount on fire, trying to force him out. To Duke Wen's consternation, he never even caught a glimpse of Jie Zitui after the fires raged for three days. Later, both Jie Zitui and his mother were found scorched under a withered willow tree. Overwhelmed with remorse, Duke Wen brought a scorched willow branch back to his court and had it made a pair of clogs. Every day, he gazed at them and sighed sadly, "Alas, thee!" Duke Wen ordered his men to bury Jie Zitui in Mount Mian and renamed it as Mount Jie. He also ordered all fires in every household to be put out on the anniversary of Jie's death to honour his memory. Thus began the Cold Food Festival, a day when no food could be cooked.

"(Jie) Zitui decided to live in seclusion. Hill fires then burnt him dead. The whole world observe the Cold Food Festival, for thousands of years just for one person." This poem entitled *Cold Food Festival* by Lu Xiang, the Tang Dynasty poet, expressed the veneration of later generations to Jie Zitui. Though the Cold Food Festival gradually spread around, not all of the people at that time were happy with the cold-food and no-fire practice. *Hou Han Shu*, or *Book of the Later Han* by Fan Ye which recorded the customs of the Cold Food Festival reads,

Zhou Ju moved to Bingzhou, present-day Taiyuan, capital city of Shanxi Province to serve as governor. In Taiyuan prefecture, the old custom regarded lighting fire as a taboo because Jie Zitui was burnt dead and said all gods and spirits were not happy with fire in the month of March, so the

Chapter One
Origin

document was sent to the Zitui Temple saying, "Since Cold Food lasted for one month, nobody, old and young alike, can stand it, so now only for three days".

Zhou Ju held the view that the cold-food practice was harmful to people physically, so he disseminated his ideas to educate his people. Coincidentally, at the end of the Eastern Han Dynasty, Cao Cao, pointed out in *Mingfa Ling*, or *Definite Punishment Order* "It was heard that fires are forbidden and therefore cold foods are eaten in places like Taiyuan, Shangdang, Xihe and Yanmen for the sake of Jie Zitui. Since it is very cold in the north, the old and young are very weak and cannot bear it. So once my order reaches, no cold food will be allowed". What Cao Cao said showed that he was not for the fire-prohibiting practice on Qingming and that it is harmful to people's health. However, this custom is still popular among the people no matter how the propaganda was done.

However, there is another saying that no fire during Cold Food Festival has something to do with ancient astronomy. The "fire" in both Hanshi and Qingming refers to what is called Big Fire Star in Chinese astronomy, that is Antares, literally "Heart Mansion Two" in Chinese. In ancient Chinese astronomy, the Seven Mansions of the East are called the Azure Dragon God, the Seven Mansions of the South called the Vermilion Bird God, the Seven Mansions of the West called the White Tiger God, and the Seven Mansions of the

日而已。"

周举认为寒食习俗伤身，并向人们宣传他的观点，以启迪民智。无独有偶，东汉末年，曹操在《明罚令》中指出，"闻太原、上党、西河、雁门冬至后百五日皆绝火寒食，云为介之推。且北方沍寒之地，老少羸弱，将有不堪之患。令到，人不得寒食"。曹操的一番话，也表明他并不赞成寒食禁火的习俗，并认为这一习俗危害人们的身体健康。但是无论怎样宣传，这一习俗仍然在民间得到传承。

但还有一种说法，寒食节的禁火与古代天文知识有关。寒食禁火和清明出火，"火"指的是天文学上的"大火星"，即"心宿二"。在古代天文知识中，东方七宿称为苍龙神，南方七宿称为朱雀神，西方七宿为白虎神，北方七宿为玄武神。大火星属二十八宿之东方苍龙

第一章 起源

七宿（包括角、亢、氐、房、心、尾、箕七宿）的第五宿心宿第二颗星，古代的人们用它来确定季节的规律。黄昏时大火星初出东方，为夏历三月，也因此成为农耕"新生活"的标志，所以就有了禁火、出火的习俗。

North called the Black Tortoise god. The Big Fire Star belongs to the second star of the fifth mansion, i.e. Heart Mansion of the Azure Dragon of the East in the Twenty-eight Mansions including the seven mansions, i.e. Horn, Neck, Root, Room, Heart, Tail and Winnowing Basket. The ancient Chinese people used it to determine the rule of the seasons. At dusk, the Big Fire Star first appeared in the east in the third month in the calendar of the Xia Dynasty, and therefore, it became the symbol of the new civilized life. As a result, the practice of banning on fire and moving of the spirit tablet came into being.

寒食节的具体日期为冬至后第105天，除了闰年，每年公历4月5日。而寒食节禁火习俗到了唐代已经由民间走向宫廷。

The Hanshi Festival falls on the 105th day after the winter solstice, April 5th by the Gregorian calendar, except in leap years. And the no-fire practice has already spread into the court during the Tang Dynasty. Based on the official regulations,

Chapter One
Origin

during the Hanshi Festival fire is forbidden for three days. In addition, different arrangements were made during these three days. The first day is big Hanshi, private Hanshi; the second day, official Hanshi, and the third day, small Hanshi. On the day right before the Hanshi Festival, people were supposed to get everything ready in advance, prepared three days' cooked food , hence the name Cooked-Food Day. On Big Hanshi Day, just as *Yunxian Zaji* by Feng Zhi during the Tang Dynasty recorded, "people in Luoyang ate cold food, decorated carriages with thousands of flowers, cooked peach flower porridge" and extinguished fire. The government sent people with chicken feather to check the hearth in every household. The whole family would be punished if the feather got scorched by the smoldering ashes. So every family had to eat cold food.

根据官方的规定，寒食节一共禁火三天，并且这三天里有不同的安排。第一天为大寒食、私寒食，第二天为官寒食，第三天为小寒食。在寒食节的前一天，人们要提前做好准备，预备好三天的熟食，所以这一天也被称为"炊熟日"。进入大寒食日以后，正如《云仙杂记》所云，"洛阳人家，寒食，装万花舆，煮杨花粥"，并灭掉火种，官府派人手持鸡毛检查各家灶灰，灰有火烬而使鸡毛发焦者，这一家人就要受到惩罚，所以家家户户只能吃冷食。

第一章 起源

禁火，是寒食节的一大特征。但节日之后，家家户户都要重新生火，生新火就成为一种辞旧迎新的过渡仪式，表达了一种季节更替的信息，也象征新的开始。三天之后的清明时节，各家各户就要取新火了，杜甫《清明》诗云："朝来新火起新烟"。唐代宫中，每到清明节，宫禁内的小孩钻榆木取火，先得火者皇帝赐绢一匹，银碗一只；取得新火，皇帝要给臣下"赐火"，以示恩宠，也表示"顺阳气"的含义（《岁时广记》）。新季节象征了新的希望和生命，所以就有了感恩的含义，表达对旧事物的怀念和感谢。因此，寒食禁火冷食祭墓，清明取新火踏青出游。

唐宋之后，寒食与清明一样，成为民间的重要假期。"春城无处不飞花，寒食东风御柳

Cessation of fire is one distinctive characteristic of the Hanshi Festival. However, after the festival, all households would make new fires which became the transitional ceremony, an expression of the information of the change of seasons, a symbol of the new beginning. So three days later after Qingming, every household was going to light a new fire, reflected in the line "On (the Qingming) morning, new fire produces new smoke" in the poem entitled *Qingming* by Du Fu, a prominent Tang Dynasty poet. Based on *Suishi Guangji* by Chen Yuanliang of the Song Dynasty, during the Tang Dynasty, whenever Qingming came, little kids in the palace were required to bore a hole in elm wood to make fire by rubbing wood pieces together. The kid who first got the fire would be given by the emperor a bolt of silk and a silver bowl as a reward. And the emperor would grant fire to his officials after obtaining new fire to show his favor and express the meaning of obedience of *Yang-qi*—the primordial masculine energies according to Taoist cosmology. The new season symbolizes new hope and life, and therefore means gratitude and expresses the memory and thanks to old stuff. Therefore, during the Hanshi Festival, no fire was allowed, cold food was eaten and the ancestral tomb was tended while during the Qingming Festival people would light new fires and go on for an outing.

After the Tang and Song Dynasties, both Hanshi and Qingming became very important holidays. "All over the Spring City flying flowers everywhere, On Cold Food Festival the east wind blew the imperial

Chapter One
Origin

willows slant. At dusk within the Han Palace candles glowed, towards the five mansions of nobility, the light smoke of the tapers flowed." This is the poem by Han Hong, a poet of the Tang Dynasty, which describes the beautiful scene of the Hanshi Festival in the Capital City of Chang'an. During Qingming and Hanshi Festivals during the reigns of different emperors, there were 4 to 7 public holidays respectively. Especially during the Song Dynasty, the special regulation was made by the government that Taixue—the Imperial College would be closed for 3 days while Wuxue—the Military School in ancient China for 1 day to allow the people to enjoy themselves to the fullest, sweep the tombs and worship their ancestors. We can also get a glimpse of the urban life and the folk customs of entertainment through the celebration of the Qingming Festival during the Song Dynasty. *Qing Ming Shang He Tu*, or *Along the River During the Qingming Festival* by the Song Dynasty artist Zhang Zeduan, presents a spectacular picture of the daily life of people and the landscape of the capital, Bianjing, today's Kaifeng, in the Qingming and Hanshi period.

After the Song and Yuan Dynasties, the Qingming Festival and Hanshi Festival were gradually merged into one. The sacrificial custom during the Hanshi Festival were also gradually emerged into those Qingming activities. In the meantime, the practice of Shangsi Spring Frolicking, actually the traditional Chinese Valentine's Day, was also mingled with Qingming activities. Generally speaking, after the Ming and Qing Dynasties, both Shangsi and Hanshi

斜。日暮汉宫传蜡烛，轻烟散入五侯家"的诗句，便是唐代诗人韩翃描写的京城寒食节的美好景象。唐代不同年号的寒食与清明，分别有四至七天时间的公共假期。尤其是宋代，官方为了让人们可以在清明时节尽情玩乐、扫墓祭祖，特地规定太学放假三日，武学放假一日。宋代都市化的生活和娱乐化的民俗，也由此可见一斑。大画家张择端所描绘的《清明上河图》也是汴京清明、寒食期间的盛世图景。

宋元之后，清明与寒食节逐渐合二为一，寒食节中的祭祀习俗也逐渐纳入清明节的活动之中。同时，上巳节"上巳春嬉"的节俗也被归到了清明节的名下。明清以后，上巳节和寒食节基本上退出了节日系统，人们只将清明

第一章 起源

节视作传统节日,"寒食不举火,祭祖先墓,设秋千以达阳气"。有些地区在清明节前一天或前两天过寒食节,还有很多地区将寒食节合并到清明节进行。如甘肃静宁州"寒食,不举火会客";河南偃师"清明前一日寒食,泊酒肴祭墓,剪纸钱挂树",邓州"清明前二日寒日,民间祭扎坟墓,添土,挂纸于颠"。很多地区将寒食节合并到清明节进行。陕西宜川县"清明戏秋千、拜坟,作馒头相馈,上缀多样虫鸟,名为介子推,谓晋文焚山,禽鸟争救子推也"。浙江云和县"清明折柳插门,谓之挂青,拜扫先茔,悬楮钱,谓之标墓,前期妇女采蓬叶和稻米为粒牧,揉作团子样,实以鸡豚之隋菹,以蔬苟调之,以饴祀先及馈戚好,可冷食,俗呼蓬果,又名蓬铸,盖禁火遗意也"。安徽泾县"插柳于门,人簪一嫩柳,谓辟邪,马牲醒扫墓,以竹悬纸钱而插焉,或取青艾为饼,存禁烟寒

Festivals faded out of the holiday system. People only regarded Qingming as one of the traditional festivals. During the Hanshi Festival, no fire was allowed. People would hold sacrificial ceremonies in front of their ancestors' tombs and set up swings to get *Yang-qi*. In some places, Hanshi Festival would be celebrated one day or two days before the Qingming Festival. In many areas, Hanshi was combined with Qingming. For example, in Jingning County, Gansu Province, "people would neither light fire nor receive guests during the Hanshi Festival". In Yanshi, Henan Province, "On Hanshi, the day before Qingming, it was a common practice to set up wine and other delicacies for memorial services at the tombs, and hang joss paper on branches". In Dengzhou, Henan Province, " On Hanshi, two days before Qingming, it was customary to sweep the tombs, add new soil to them, offer sacrifices to the ancestors, and hang spirit money on top of the graves. In many areas, Hanshi was merged into Qingming. In Yichuan County, Shannxi Province, there were various activities on Qingming such as riding on swings, cleaning the tomb and paying respect to the dead with offerings, making buns to give people as gifts on which a variety of insects and birds were carved named Jie Zitui, meaning that Duke Wen of the state of Jin had the Mount set on fire and countless birds flew to Zitui's rescue. In Yunhe County, Zhejiang Province, during the Qingming Festival, "willow branches were plucked and inserted into gates, called hanging greenery, sweep the tombs and offer sacrifices to

Chapter One　Origin

the ancestors, hanging paper resembling money. In former times, women would collect some raspberry leaves and rice, knead them into balls, using poultry or pork mixed with vegetables as fillings to present to the ancestors or give them to friends and relatives as gifts. Also known as Pengguo (raspberry fruit) or Pengzhu (raspberry casting), the balls can be eaten when cold, maybe some idea left over by fire forbidden". In Jingxian County, Anhui Province, "willow branches were hung up at the doorway, women would wear a tender willow branch on the head in order to ward off evils. Once animals awoke, people would go out to sweep tombs, hang paper money on tobacco poles and insert it into the tomb or make cakes out of green mugwort, which means no fire and cold food only". In Xing'an County, Jiangxi Province, "women were not allowed to sweep tombs but grind rice to make cakes, which was still the practice of the Hanshi Festival". And in Yongzhou, Hunan Province, "during the Qingming Festival, willow branches were put on doors, food and drink were prepared for tending tombs, and paper money were hung on trees, called hanging greenery".

In fact, there are distinct differences between the Hanshi Festival and the Qingming Festival. No fire was allowed during the Hanshi Festival in some places. For example, in Jingning, Gansu Province, neither lighting fire nor receiving guests was allowed. And during the Qingming Festival, "the ancestral tomb would be tended". However, more regions differed from this. On Hanshi, tombs would

食之意"。江西兴安县"妇女不上坟，粉米作粿，谓之饭粿，仍寒食之风"。湖南永州"清明节插柳于门，具酒肴登陇墓，以楮钱挂树，曰挂青"。

事实上，寒食节与清明节的区别很明显。一些地方的寒食节禁火，例如甘肃静宁州寒食节不举火、会客，清明节要"拜扫先茔"。但更多的地区与此不同，寒食节祭扫坟墓(野祭)，添土挂纸钱，

第一章 起源

做专门食品冷食；清明节折柳枝插头，或玩秋千。可见寒食是为了纪念，清明是为娱乐，当然在清明节与寒食节合而为一的地区，就看不出区别了。

be swept, fresh soil added, joss paper hung and specific cold foods were made, hence the name field offerings. While on Qingming, people would pluck willow branches and put them on the head or play on the swing. So we can see that the observance of Hanshi is to remember the ancestors while the celebration of Qingming is for entertainment. Of course, we can see no difference in those areas where Qingming and Hanshi were merged into as one.

Chapter One
Origin

3 祭 祖
Ancestor Worship

The practice of sweeping tombs and offering sacrifices to the ancestors on Qingming also has something to do with reverence and worship for ghosts and ancestors in ancient China. *Li Ji*, or *The Book of Rites* one of the Five Classics of the Confucian canon, reads, "Everything that grows between Heaven and Earth is called Life. Its death is called *Zhe*. Dead people are called ghosts. This remained the same for five generations until the seventh generation. What is new is that the ancestors were worshipped at the grave site. The rest remained unchanged." That is to say, everything has both the beginning and the end. People become ghosts after death. When a person dies, the body perishes but the soul still exists, as recorded in *Li Ji*, "the spirit goes back to Heaven while the body goes back to Earth". Therefore, the dead ancestors must be worshipped.

清明节扫墓祭祖的习俗还与中国古代对鬼魂的敬畏以及对祖先的崇敬之礼有关。《礼记·祭法》云"大凡生于天地之间者皆曰命。其万物死皆曰折。人死曰鬼。此五代之所不变也。七代之所更立者。禘郊宗祖。其余不变也",即是说天地万物皆有始有终,人死去之后就变成鬼了,肉体虽灭,但鬼魂犹存。"魂气归于天,形魄归于地"(《礼记·郊特牲》),所以需要对逝去的先人进行祭拜。如果不祭拜,就会招

第一章 起源

来魂灵的反击。例如一个著名的故事所言：

> 周宣王杀其臣杜伯而不辜，杜伯曰："吾君杀我而不辜，若以死者为无知，则止矣。若死而有知，不出三年，必使吾君知之。"其三年，周宣王合诸侯而田于圃田，车数百乘，从数千，人满野。日中，杜伯乘白马素车，朱衣冠，执朱弓，挟朱矢，追周宣王，射之车上，中心折脊，殪车中，伏弢而死。

周宣王遇到杜伯的鬼魂对他施以报复，最后身亡。这也反映出先秦时的人们对待鬼魂的态度。人们认为鬼魂普遍存在，因而与活人有血缘关系的鬼魂受到崇拜，成为祖先神。因此，春季的祭礼表达了对祖先以及天地的祭拜，《礼记·祭统》："凡祭有四时：春祭曰礿，夏祭曰禘，秋祭曰

If no sacrifices were offered to the dead, they will take revenge. Here is a famous story:

King Xuan, the eleventh king of the Zhou Dynasty, killed his innocent minister called Du Bo. Before he died, Du Bo said, "My Lord is killing me even though I am completely guiltless. If the dead is unconscious, then that is the end of it. If the dead is conscious, then within three years' time, my Lord shall know of this!" Three years later, King Xuan together with his officials went hunting in the wilds. There were several hundred chariots and several thousand men on foot. The hunting party filled the entire field. At noon, Du Bo appeared in a plain chariot pulled by white horses. He was wearing vermillion clothes and a hat, holding a vermillion row, and clasping vermillion arrows under his arm. He chased after King Xuan and shot him as he rode in his chariot. The arrow pieced the heart of King Xuan and splintered his spine. King Xuan collapsed in his chariot, draped over his own bow case, died.

King Xuan encountered Du Bo's ghost who took revenge on him and killed him eventually. This story is a reflection of the Pre-Qin people's attitude towards ghosts. It was a common view that ghosts and spirits are omniscient, therefore ghosts become the Ancestor God and get worshipped due to their blood relationship with the living. Therefore, spring offerings were the expression of worship of ancestors, Heaven and Earth. *Li Ji* reads, "Sacrificial offerings were made in four seasons. Spring Offering is called *Yue* (sacrifice). Summer Offering is called *Di* (imperial ancestor worship),

Chapter One
Origin

Fall Offering is called *Chang* (experience). Winter Offering is called *Zheng*." *Li Ji* also says, "In spring and autumn, ancestors' temples were renovated, ceremonial utensils were set up, clothes were made, and seasonal foods were offered." That is to say, in both spring and autumn, ceremonial services were held to pay respect to the ancestors, which is similar to festive offerings. In the Western Zhou Dynasty, great importance was attached to tomb burial. Mencius of the Warring States Period also mentioned in his *Mengzi* that "A native of the State of Qi, one of the many vassal states of the Zhou Dynasty, eventually walked to the grave site outside of the eastern city and went over to the tomb sweepers begging for some leftovers. Not enough, he looked around and ran to somewhere else begging. This is how he got full and drunk." This laughing stock often went to the grave outside of the eastern city to beg for offerings, from which we can see that the tomb sweeping practice was very popular during the Warring States Period.

The reverence for ancestors and praying for their protection leads to the combination of the sacrificial

尝，冬祭日烝。"《礼记·中庸》："春秋，修其祖庙，陈其宗器，设其衣裳，荐其时食。"也就是说，春秋两季要祭祀先祖，与节庆祭祀类似。在西周时对墓葬就十分重视。东周战国时代《孟子·齐人篇》也曾提及"卒之东郭墦间之祭者乞其馀，不足，又顾而之他。此其为餍足之道也"，说的是一个为人所耻笑的齐国人，常到东郭坟墓乞食祭墓的祭品。可见战国时代扫墓之风气十分盛行。

对祖先的敬畏和祈求保佑的心态，使得祭礼逐

第一章 起源

渐与寒食节的活动融合在一起。禁火是为了出火，祭亡是为了佑生。唐代以前，寒食节怀旧悼亡，清明节求新护生，两个节日代表了阴阳相息的关系。在唐代，官方下令把民间扫墓的风俗固定在寒食节，但后来因为寒食节与清明节前后相连，扫墓也由寒食节顺延到了清明。

清代，清明节的主要内容依然是扫墓，为祖先的坟墓除草添土，在树枝上挂些纸钱和纸条，焚烧纸钱，寄托对祖先的哀思。除此之外，在聚族而居的地区，还要在宗族祠堂里举行祭祀祖先的活动，将族人召集到祠堂一起祭拜亡者，再将一些祭祀品分发给族人。另外，清明节的时候还要折下柳枝戴在头上，当时还有说法是"清明不戴柳，来生变黄狗"，因为柳树有辟邪的功能。另外一种说法，插柳的风俗是为了纪念"教民稼穑"的农事祖

rites and the activities during the Hanshi Festival. The fire-forbidden practice was to more the spirit tablet while the sacrificial offerings to the dead was to protect the living. Before the Tang Dynasty, the Hanshi Festival was observed to look back and commemorate the dead while the Qingming Festival was to pray for the new and protect the living. Therefore, the two festivals represent the circular relationship between *Yin* and *Yang*. During the Tang Dynasty, the civil practice of tomb sweeping was fixed by the government during the Hanshi Festival. But later, the tomb-sweeping practice was extended till the Qingming Festival since Hanshi and Qingming were adjacent in time.

During the Qing Dynasty, the most important activity to do during the Qingming Festival was still to sweep the tombs, get rid of weeds, add new soil to the graves, hang joss paper and strips on branches and burn the spirit money in memory of the ancestors. Apart from this, in those places where the whole clan family live together, the ceremonial services for worshipping the ancestors would be held in the ancestral temple. The clansmen would be called together to offer sacrifices to the deceased. And some sacrifices would be distributed among them afterwards. In addition, people would pluck willow branches to put on head. There was a saying, "You will be reincarnated into a yellow dog in the next life if not wearing willow branches on Qingming" because willow trees have the function of warding off evils. Another saying goes that the custom of inserting willow branches is in memory

Chapter One
Origin

of Hou Ji, the ancestor of agriculture who taught people farming. Mencius once said, "Hou Ji taught people husbandry, and to recognize the five grains. When the five grains ripe, people get fed up."

The forefather of the Zhou Dynasty was called Hou Ji. His nickname was Qi (throw away). His mother's name was Jiang Yuan. Jiang Yuan stamped into a giant's footprint, got pregnant and gave birth to a boy after a whole year. Considering it unlucky, she wanted to desert the baby but in vain. Amazed by her son, Jiang Yuan brought the baby back home and raised him up. Hou Ji liked planting very much at a very young age. After he grew up, he was even more fond of farming and always ready to teach people how to do farming. Hou Ji brought all kinds of seeds from Heaven and disseminated them into the human world. The big harvests made agriculture prosperous.

In memory of Hou Ji who taught people farming, the later generations would put willow branches on the head on Qingming when they offered sacrifices and pay respect to their ancestors to pray for blessings and peace, and ward off evils and spirits. In addition, in some places in Shaanxi Province, dough tigers flours were used to get rid of evils during the Qingming Festival. Also in some areas, little kids would wear Qingming strands made of mugwort leaves and red cloth strips during the Qingming Festival. A kind of mugwort cakes were also made out of the juice of mugwort leaves to keep off evils. A very moving story was very popular

师后稷。孟子曰："后稷教民稼穑，树艺五谷，五谷熟而民人育。"

周代的先民后稷，名字叫弃，他的母亲叫姜原。姜原在野外踩到了一个巨人的脚印，因此而怀孕，过了整整一年才生下个男孩。她认为不吉利，想抛弃孩子，但没有成功。姜原感到儿子很神奇，就把他抱回家养大了。后稷小时候喜欢栽麻种豆，长大了更爱好农耕，教百姓干农活。后稷从天上拿来百谷的种子播撒人间，结出丰硕的果实，推动了农业的繁荣。

后人为了纪念后稷教民稼穑，在清明祭祖的时候就折下柳枝戴在头上，表达对先祖的哀悼和崇敬之情，以及祈求先祖保佑平安、镇邪驱鬼的愿景。此外，陕西一带在清明期间则用面塑老虎来辟邪。还有一些地方，清明节的时候要用艾叶和红布条扎成"清明穗"给小孩子戴上，同时还制作一种艾蒿的叶汁和面的艾糕，说是

第一章 起源

辟邪。当地还流传了一个动人的故事呢！

相传很早以前，梁东一带本是荒草滩，每逢雨水旺的年头，这里便滋生出许多蚊虫，人畜遭到叮咬后，就会生一种"黑斑病"。生了这种病，先黑头脚，再黑四肢，待全身发黑之后，生命就没有指望了。所以，很久以来，没人敢到这里落户，这一片肥美的草滩就一直搁荒着。

有一年刚打春的时候，从外地来了一对逃荒的小夫妻看到这一片黑油油的土地、一汪汪清亮亮的泉水，他们心动了，就在这儿住下了。丈夫艾艾，是个种田的行家。他起早贪黑，在荒草滩上平整了几亩地，撒下种子，不久便齐刷刷地长出了一片好庄稼。妻子蒿蒿，是个治家的里手。她每天砍柴编筐，拿到集市上卖掉，换些油盐酱醋、针头线脑回来。第二年清明节他们还生了一个胖小子，夫妻俩给孩子取名叫"清明"。一家人日子过得虽

among the local people:

It is said that long, long ago, the area in the east of the Central Plains was originally a vast deserted grassland. Whenever there was enough rain, there would gather countless mosquitoes. Anyone after being bit by the mosquito bite would suffer from a disease called Black Spot Disease. When a person was attacked by this disease, his/her head and feet would become black first, then the limbs, and he/she would die when it was black all over the body. As a result, for a long time, no one dared to settle down there and the vast fertile grassland remained deserted.

One year, when spring just came back, a young couple fled there from a famine-stricken area. At the sight of the rich soil and clear spring waters, they decided to settle down. Ai Ai, the husband, was a farming expert. Every day he worked very hard from dawn to dusk. He leveled several acres of grassland and sowed seeds. And very soon grew a stretch of a good cropland. Hao Hao, the wife, was an excellent housekeeper. Every day, she cut firewoods, wove baskets and sold them in the market for daily necessities. On Qingming next year, she gave birth to a chubby boy who was given the name Qing Ming by his parents. They were not rich but pretty happy.

Chapter One
Origin

Good days are always short. On their third year there, the sunny weather turned hostile all of a sudden as soon as spring began. And rain fell on the earth for forty-nine consecutive days. As a result, earth sank, caves collapsed, and mosquitoes started to wreak havoc. They flew out of ditches and thick grass, biting everywhere. So both Ai Ai and Hao Hao were infected by Black Spot Disease. In order to keep a male descendant, they gave their little kid to a passerby. Soon they died from illness. Touched by their daily deep love, their villagers buried them together. From then on, there were even fewer people coming here.

Twenty years had passed in a twinkling. On Qingming one year, another young couple came to visit a grave to honor the memory of their beloved deceased. It turned out that Qing Ming married the daughter of his adoptive parents when he grew up. On the second day of their marriage, Qing Ming brought his wife to visit his own parents' tomb. They were struck dumb when they came to the grave. It was Qingming period, still too early for a truly beautiful spring scene. However, at the head of the tomb grew a kind of unnamable grass, luxuriant and exotically fragrant. The young couple moved this cluster of grass to their yard in memory of their parents.

不宽裕，但也和和美美。

谁知好景不长。第三年一开春，晴朗朗的天忽然变了脸，一场雨下了七七四十九天。地陷了，窑塌了，蚊虫开始肆虐了。它们从水沟里、草丛里钻出来，乱叮乱咬。艾艾和蒿蒿都染上了黑斑病。为了留下一条根，他们将孩子交给一个过路人带走了。不久，这夫妻俩都病死了。附近的乡亲们感念他们平时的恩爱，把他们合葬了。从此以后，这一带更少有人来了。

一晃二十年过去了。一年清明时节，这里又来了一对小夫妻，是来上坟的。原来，清明长大成人后，和抚养人的女儿结了婚。婚后的第二天，清明便带了妻子来给父母上坟。来到坟前一看，他们不由得愣住了：清明时节，还不到花红柳绿的时候，这坟头上却长了一墩叫不出名的草，郁郁葱葱，还散发出一股奇异的香气。这对小夫妻为了寄托对父母的思

第一章 起源

念，便将这墩草移到自家的院里栽上了。

就在这一年，黑斑病又蔓延开来，村里不少人家都染了病，唯独清明家，连一只蚊子也没有，更不用说什么黑斑病了。乡亲们说，这是清明的父母显灵了，用这墩草把清明护住了。清明夫妻便摘下一些叶片送给人们治病，居然真的把黑斑病治好了。人们看到这草这样神奇，便将它奉为珍宝，家家户户移栽起来，并给它起了名字叫"艾蒿"。每逢清明节的时候，便掐一段艾蒿，扎上"角红布"戴在孩子们的头上，称为"清明穗"，用以避邪，慢慢地形成了习惯。这两种古老的习俗一直延续到今。

在清末，庙祭都是全族的大祭祀活动，一般

Just in this year, Black Spot Disease spread again. As a result, quite a lot of villagers caught this disease. However, not a single mosquito could be found in Qing Ming's house, let alone Black Spot Disease. Everybody in the village said that Qing Ming's escape from the disaster was thanks to manifestation of his parents. So the couple plucked some grass leaves to give the people, which stopped the disease unexpectedly. Because of the magic function of the grass, it was treasured, and planted in every household, and was named after the couple as Ai Hao. From then on, when the Qingming Festival came, adults would nip off a segment of Ai Hao, wind a piece of red cloth onto it, and put them on the heads of their children, called Qingming Tassel, to ward off evils, which gradually developed into a custom. These two practices continue to date.

At the end of the Qing Dynasty, the temple offering was a big sacrificial ceremony to the entire

Chapter One
Origin

clan. Generally speaking, it was held every year during the Qingming Festival, the Festival of the Dead Spirits (15th day of the 7th lunar month when sacrifices are offered to the dead), Winter Solstice, the first day of the first lunar month, and the anniversary of the death of the remote ancestors as well. The times and contents of the sacrificial ceremonies differed in different places, but they had something in common, that is, the same clan belonged to the same temple. And there were definite regulations for the sacrificial ceremonies, set-ups and financial arrangements. For example, *Zongci Banji Guize*, or *Rules and Regulations for Ancestral Hall Sacrificial Offerings* of Luo's clan in Gusangzhou, Xiangtan County, Hunan Province reads,

Spring Offering was originally held on the 15th day of the lunar 3rd month, now Qingming is set as a fixed annual Spring offering. Since the ceremony just started, there were very few clansmen attending the rites, so it is not necessary for four people in charge as in the past. Winter Offering is fixed on the 2nd day of the lunar 10th month. Since everything was finished, people near and far, will get together. As a result, it is extremely money-consuming, so all four halls should be used. In the years of Si, You and Chou, the ceremony shall be held in Xinwu Hall, in the years of Yin, Wu and Xu, in Hutian Hall, in the years of Hai, Mao and Wei, in Dushang Hall, and in the years of Shen, Zi and Chen, in Jueshang Hall. Though we have four halls, we have only one ceremony. Everyone is supposed to try his best and be united as one to avoid show-off."

在每年的清明、中元、冬至、大年初一和远祖忌诞日举行，各地祭祖时间和内容有所不同，但以祠堂为一族，对于祭祀仪式、设置和经费安排都有明文规定。例如湘潭县鼓磉洲罗氏的《宗祠办祭规则》就规定：

春祭原期三月十五日，近改清明日为每年春祭定期。东作方兴，与祭者恒少，故止当年四人办理；冬祭定期十月初二日，万宝告成，远近毕集，费用浩繁，故分四堂办理：凡巳、酉、丑年新屋堂办，寅、午、戌年湖田堂办，亥、卯、未年杜山堂办，申、子、辰年蕨山堂办。堂虽分四，祭则为一，务宜尽志尽物，恪供祭典，不得分彼此以相夸耀。

第一章 起源

4 节气
Solar Nodes or Terms

虽然作为节日的清明在唐朝才形成，但作为时序标志的清明节气早已被古人所认识，汉代已有了明确的记载。清明与节气的关系，源自于"八风"的传说。八风是我国古代最早区分季候风的方式。根据《吕氏春秋》记载，一年之间每间隔约45天，就吹不同的风。从冬至算起，依序是北方寒风、东北炎风、东方滔风、东南熏风（清明风）、南方巨风、西南凄风等，于是清明成

Though Qingming did not come into being as a holiday until the Tang Dynasty, it has long been well known as a solar term to the ancient Chinese, which was definitely recorded as early as the Han Dynasty. The relationship between Qingming and the solar terms originated from the folk tale of Ba Feng, or Eight Winds which is the earliest way to distinguish seasonal winds in ancient China. Based on *Lüshi Chunqiu*, or *Mister Lü's Spring and Autumn Annals*, an encyclopedic Chinese classic text, at the interval of about 45 days within one year, different winds blow. Starting from the Winter Solstice, the eight winds blowing in order are Cold North Wind, Hot Northeasterly Wind, Torrential East Wind, Southeasterly Warm Breeze (Qingming Wind), South Gale, Southwesterly Wailing Wind and so on. Therefore, Qingming became one of the signs of the

Chapter One
Origin

climate. Qingming as one of the 24 solar terms was much earlier than the Qingming Festival as a civilian holiday. Qingming is one of the 24 solar terms, between the middle and late spring, that is on the 106th day after the Winter Soltice. The numbering of days based on the Gan-Zhi (Heavenly Stems and Earthly Branches) calendar system and the division of one year into 24 solar terms began from the Yin Dynasty and Zhou Dynasty respectively. And Qingming as one of the solar terms probably started from the Zhou Dynasty. And the earliest record in writing about Qingming can be seen in *Huainanzi: Tianwen Xun*, literally *The Masters/Philosophers of Huainan: Patterns of Heaven*, compiled by Liu An of the Western Han Dynasty. It says, "On the 15th day from the Spring Equinox, the sun is exactly at the celestial longitude of 345°, it is called Qingming" which falls on April 4th or 5th each year on the Gregorean calendar. Chen Yuanliang, the Song period scholar recorded in *Suishi Guangji*, or *Vast Records of the Annual Seasons*, an overview of the imperial edicts pronounced regularly according to the annual seasons, "Qingming means things are clean and bright". Qingming is a busy rainy season for both plowing and planting.

It is well-known that the lunar 24 Solar Nodes are closely related to agrarian life in China. When Qingming comes, the temperature is rising, flowers are blossoming, trees are budding, it is indeed a good time for plowing and planting. No wonder there is a saying, "plant melons and beans around Qingming".

为气候的标记之一。作为农历二十四节气的清明，远早于成为民俗节日的清明节。清明是农历二十四节气之一，在仲春与暮春之交，也就是冬至后的第106天。以干支记日和将一年划分为二十四节气，分别开始于殷代和周代。作为节气的清明，大约始于周代。关于清明最早的文字记载，是西汉刘安所编的《淮南子·天文训》，它说"春分后十五日，斗指乙，为清明"，时间是每年公历的4月4日或5日。宋代的陈元靓在《岁时广记·三统历》中记载"清明者，谓物生清净明洁"。清明是多雨时节，也是春耕、春种的大忙时节。

众所周知，农历二十四节气与我国农耕生活密切相关。清明一到，气温升高，正是春耕春种的大好时节，春暖花开，柳枝吐芽，故有"清明前后，种瓜种豆"之说。

第一章 起源

　　在二十四个节气中，既是节气又是节日的只有清明（冬至在历史上也是一个节日，但现在各地大多不再过此节）。此外，民间的一些重要活动都安排在清明前后，作为一个辞旧迎新的时间标记。例如"青岗县房地收赎都要求在清明以前"，"河南开封民间有'三不回春、八不回秋'（收赎应在清明前、秋收后）或'当白回白，当青回青'（收赎时土地状况应和出典时状况相同）的习惯"，"涞源县又有'三不得麦，六不得秋'的说法，限制收赎在清明前及农历六月六日前"。

　　清明与蚕事最初的

Among the 24 solar terms, only Qingming is also a holiday. In history, the winter solstice was also a holiday, but now it is not observed in most regions any longer. In addition, some important civil activities are arranged without any exception before or after Qingming as a time sign of biding farewell to the old year and ushering in the new. Here are some examples. In Qinggang County, Heilongjiang Province, redemption of the fields must be done before Qingming. There were practices in Kaifeng City, Henan Province, that redemption should be done before Qingming and after the autumn harvest and that the soil condition on the day of redemption should be the same as that on the day of purchase. And in Laiyuan County, Hebei Province, redemption was required to be done before Qingming and before the lunar June 6th.

The initial function of Qingming and silkworm

Chapter One
Origin

raising were originally related to agricultural activities. Cui Shi, the Eastern Han Dynasty scholar, recorded in his *Simin Yueling*, or *The Monthly Decretes to the Four [Groups of] People*, an agricultural treatise from the Later Han Period, "On Qingming Festival, female silkworm breeders were ordered to take care of the silkworm containers, get rid of holes and prepare for wooden posts and rice". We can see that not only is Qingming related to farming, it also has something to do with sericulture about which there is a beautiful story among the people as follows:

Long time ago, there lived a rich family in a mulberry field at a watery town. The father died young, leaving only the mother and daughter depending on each other. Mrs. Liu, the mother, was born hot-tempered. She feared the wicked but bullied the kind while Cuihua, the daughter, was kind, gentle and as beautiful as flowers. Her beauty drew many talented suitors to their house but all of them were rejected by the snobbish mother who bit off more than she can chew. But one day a gang of bandits kidnapped Cuihua, Mrs. Liu could do nothing but burn the joss sticks to beg for Buddha. She vowed to Heaven, "I'll marry my daughter to whoever can save her". Unexpectedly, their big white horse happened to hear her words. In fact, this white horse was a divine one. It saved Cuihua. But not only did Mrs. Liu deny what she had said, she also shot the large white horse dead. Conscious of what happened, Cuihua could not help shedding tears. She had the idea of going to

功能与农事活动有关。东汉崔寔《四民月令》记载："清明节，命蚕妾，治蚕室，除隙穴，具槌持。"清明不仅与农耕相关，也与蚕事有关。而关于蚕事，民间有一个这样的传说：

很久以前在水乡桑园中有一大户人家，因父亲早逝，只留下母女俩相依为命。母亲刘氏生性暴戾，惧恶欺善，女儿翠花善良温柔，且貌美如花。许多才子前来求婚，都被欺贫爱富、好高骛远的刘氏拒绝了。但有一天一伙强盗掳走了翠花，刘氏万般无奈唯有烧香求佛，对天发誓："无论是谁，只要能救出我女儿，我就把女儿嫁给他。"她家的大白马正巧听到了她的话。其实这匹大白马是一匹神马，它把翠花救了出来，可刘氏不仅矢口否认自己当初说过的话，还将大白马射死了。翠花知道了，

第一章 起源

流着泪想去院子把暴晒在外的马皮收藏起来。刚走进院子，那张雪白的马皮被一阵狂风吹起，直扑她而来，卷起了她向天上飞去。等四邻们都赶来时，那裹着翠花的马皮又从空中飘飘悠悠地坠落在了一棵桑树上。刘氏和众乡邻急忙奔过去，只见翠花姑娘已变成了一条浑身雪白、马头模样的虫子，此时她正爬到树上，扭动着身子，嘴里不停地吐出亮晶晶的细丝绞缠自己呢。

the yard to collect and hide the horsehide exposed to the sun. No sooner had she walked into the yard than a gust of wind blew the snow-white horsehide up, sprang on her and rolled her up to the sky. After all the neighbors rushed there, the horsehide in which Cuihua was wrapped fell on a mulberry tree, fluttering leisurely. Mrs. Liu and all the neighbors ran hastily there only to see that Cuihua has become a snow-white-bodied, horse-headed worm. At that time, it was climbing on the tree, writhing its body, and its mouth kept spitting out shiny filaments, twisting and tangling itself.

Chapter One
Origin

Since then, a new animal, called "silkworm" appeared in the world. It is said that the Chinese character of silkworm evolved from the character "can" meaning "tangle together". At the same time, the tree which Cuihua inhabited after death is called "sang" (mulberry) also because in Chinese the funeral character is homophonic with the mulberry character. Later, silkworms were raised for reeling silk, spinning, weaving and sewing clothes as well as keeping out cold in winter. And later on, in order to express their sincere gratitude towards the Silk Flower Princess and the white horse for the great favor, the local people donated to build a Silk Flower Temple on top of the Mount Han, Ma'anshan City, Anhui Province, in which the sculptures of the Silk Flower Princess and the white horse are enshrined and worshipped. Whenever the Qingming Festival comes, the sericulturists, near and far alike, come to worship, praying for silkworm flower harvest.

It is said that the lunar March 16th is the birthday of the Silkworm Flower Goddess in the folklore. On this day, the silkworm breeders will hold the solemn ceremony of worshipping the Silkworm Goddess and boating races such as riding a white ship, a benchmark boat, and a boxing ship, etc. And the Flower Drum performances were also offered. Later, these activities were incorporated into the celebration of the Qingming Festival.

As one of the 24 solar nodes, Qingming is also one of the labels to ward off evils. Based on the records in *Gujin Tushu Jicheng*, literally *Complete*

从此，世界上有了一种新的动物，叫作"蚕"。据说蚕就是由"缠"字引申而来的；同时，姑娘丧命后所栖落的那种树叫作"桑"，也是因为桑跟"丧"谐音的缘故。后来，人们都将蚕宝宝饲养起来，缫丝、纺织，用来缝衣服，冬天可以御寒。再后来，人们为了感激蚕花公主和白马的恩赐，捐资在含山顶上修建了一座蚕花殿，供上蚕花公主和白马的雕塑，每逢清明节，远近蚕农都前来朝拜，祈祷蚕花丰收。

民间传说每年的三月十六是蚕花娘娘的生日。在这一天，蚕农们要举行隆重的祀蚕神仪式，还要举行花鼓戏表演和踏白船、标杆船、打拳船等竞赛。后来，这些活动被合并到清明节中举行。

清明作为节气，还是避邪的标签之一。根据《古今图书集成》记载，

第一章 起源

宋代陈自明"胎煞避忌产前将护法"中有一种按农时节气分定胎煞位置的办法，其文曰："月游胎煞：立春在房床，惊蛰在户，清明在门，立夏在灶，芒种在母身，小暑在灶，立秋在碓，白露在厨前，寒露在门，立冬在户及厨，大雪在炉及灶，小寒在房母身。"

Collection of Illustrations and Writings from the Earliest to Current Times, a vast encyclopaedic work written in China during the reigns of Qing emperors Kangxi and Yongzheng, there is a method in *the Prenatal Protection Rule for the Fetus Demon Taboos* by Chen Ziming, a well-known doctor of the Song Dynasty in determining the positions of the Fetus Fiend according to the farming seasons and solar nodes. The text reads, "the Fetus Evil moves on a monthly basis: on Lichun (the inception of spring, around Feb. 5th), it is in the bed; on Jingzhe (awakening of hibernated insects, around March 5th), it is on the window; on Qingming (clear and bright, around April 5th), it is on the door; on Lixia (start of summer, around May 5th), it is on the kitchen range; on Mangzhong (grain in ear, around June 6th), it is in the mother's body; on Xiaoshu (minor heat, around July 7th), it is also on the kitchen range; on Liqiu (start of autumn, Aug. 7th), it is on the hammer; on Bailu (white dew, around Sept. 7th), it is in the front of the kitchen; on Hanlu (cold dew, around Oct. 8th), it is also on the door; on Lidong (start of winter), it is on the window and in the kitchen; on Daxue (major snow, around Dec. 7th), it is on the cooking range; on Xiaohan (minor cold, around Jan. 5th), it is in the house and the mother's body."

Chapter One
Origin

5 清明节
The Qingming Festival

Just as we mentioned before, Qingming, as a holiday, was in the embryonic stage during the Tang Dynasty. The Hanshi Festival is several days earlier than the Qingming Festival. Later, the former was integrated into the latter. The Tang Dynasty poet Zhang Ji depicts the rural idyllic picture of the Tomb Sweeping Festival in his poem entitled *Lümen Jishi*, as follows, "Farmers recruited as soldiers are on board, thousands of acres of deserted fields are dominated by green grass. You may ascend Wu Gate to look around, new Qingming smoke is rising from how many households!" The Qingming Festival was prevalent during the Song Dynasty. Wang Yuqiao in his poem entitled *Qingming* depicts his mood during the Qingming Festival. It reads, "No flowers, no wine, this is the Qingming Festival of mine. So boring, so cheerless just as a wandering monk's one. I borrowed some new fire from my neighbour yesterday for I

正如前文所述，清明作为节日，萌芽于唐代，清明前几日为寒食节，后来寒食节又与清明节融为一体。唐代诗人张继在《阊门即事》中描绘了清明时节的乡村田园画卷"耕夫召募爱楼船，春草青青万项田。试上吴门窥郡郭，清明几处有新烟"。清明节盛行于宋代，文人王禹偁在《清明》中讲述了人们度过清明节的心情，"无花无酒过清明，兴味萧然似野僧。昨日邻家乞新火，晓窗分与读书灯"。民间多于清明前后祭扫，上坟

第一章 起源

祭扫的时间，各处俗规惯习不一。《中华全国风俗志·江苏》云："清明日各家扫墓。如有新丧者，必于春秋社前三日上坟致祭……不能捎带着办其他的事情，更忌讳拐弯探访亲友。"民国《偃师县风土纪略》云"清明以前，各家多上坟者，故以清明谓'拜扫节'。"四川《涪陵县续修涪州志》云"清明上冢，标纸钱，曰挂亲"，即在清明节墓祭时修墓铲草等。清明墓祭除供酒食、燃纸、添土、扫墓等以外，还有标祀，其所用纸幡等即为"清明吊"，也称"清明吊子"。清同治《长阳县志》云："季春清明，士女踏青，以五色纸幡、各种花样，名'清明吊'，系小长竹竿插冢上，曰'插青'。"

had to get up very early to study." Handed down from ancient times to date, tomb sweeping usually takes place around Qingming, but the custom and time of tending to the graves of the departed ones vary in different places. *Zhonghua Quanguo Fengsuzhi: Jiangsu* reads, "On Qingming, each family needed to sweep the graves of their ancestors. A newly deceased must be offered sacrifices respectfully at the grave three days before spring and autumn offerings. Nothing else can be done, let alone making up excuses to visit friends and relatives." *Yanshi County Fengtu Jilüe* during the period of the Republic of China (1912—1949) says, "Before Qingming, a lot of families visited the grave sites to cherish the memory of their beloved dead, so Qingming is also called 'Tomb Visiting and Sweeping Festival'". The Sichuan Province *Weisuo County Xuxiu Fuzhou Zhi* says, "On Qingming, tombs were swept and paper money were burnt, which is called Gua Qin, literally 'full of concern about one's relatives'. That is to say, when the sacrificial ceremony is held at the grave site, the celebrants usually tend the tombs and get rid of weeds to remember and honour their ancestors. During the Qingming Festival, when a memorial ceremony is held at the grave site, apart from offering food and wine, burning joss paper, adding new soil and sweeping the tombs, there was also Biaosi in which paper banners, usually called Qingming Diao(zi) are used. *Changyang County Annals* during the reign of Emperor Tongzhi of the Qing Dynasty says, "During the Qingming Festival in the third lunar month, men and women go outside and enjoy the greenery of springtime. They would tie all kinds of five-colored

Chapter One
Origin

paper streamers to long bamboo rods and insert them into the tombs, which is called Cha Qing, literally 'insert greenery'".

In some places, there is a practice of plucking willow branches and sticking a willow twig in one's sideburns, which is related to ancestor worship. They say that "one would be reincarnated into a pig or dog after death" if not wearing willow branches. One story goes that the practice of wearing willow branches during the Qingming Festival has something to do with the peasant uprising led by Huang Chao, the leader of the Huang Chao Rebellion. In his *Chunming Suishi Suoji*, Rang Lian of the Qing Dynasty says, "Without wearing willow branches during the Qingming Festival, you will die in the hands of Huang Chao." When planning the rebellion, Huang Chao set Qingming as the date, and wearing willow branches as the sign. In Yangzhou, Jiangsu Province, there were Southern and Northern Willow Alleys. Legend has it that when Huang Chao rebelled, touched by a chivalrous woman who saved her nephew at the expense of her own son, his followers asked her to plug willow branches in front of the gates as a sign to avoid being killed by the soldiers. Therefore, the above-mentioned proverb spread among the masses. In addition, in some places during the Qingming Festival, people exchanged gifts, just as recorded in *Zanhuang County Annals* in the period of the Republic of China, "During the Qingming Festival...Man's family would give his wife's family hairpins and earrings as gifts, so the Qingming Festival is also called Zhui Jie, literally (gift) giving and receiving festival".

有些地方的习俗是清明要折柳戴柳，与祭祖有关，不戴柳者"死了变猪狗"。有一说，以为清明戴柳的习俗与黄巢造反有关，清人让廉《春明岁时琐记》中云："清明不带柳，死在黄巢手。"黄巢造反时，以清明日为期，戴柳为号。扬州旧时就有南（北）柳巷，据说是黄巢造反时，一仗义妇女宁保侄儿、弃亲子性命于不顾，因而感动了黄巢部下，嘱其门上插柳为记号而免受黄巢军士杀戮，所以就有此谚语流传。此外，还有一些地方在清明节时馈赠礼物，如民国《赞皇县志》云："清明……姻亲馈送女家簪珥，俗名'赞节'。"

第一章 起源

总之，清明节是中国最重要的传统节日之一。它不仅是人们祭奠祖先、缅怀先人的节日，也是中华民族认祖归宗的纽带，更是一个远足踏青、亲近自然、催护新生的春季仪式。与其他传统大节不一样，清明节是融合了节气与节俗的综合节日。作为清明节重要节日内容的祭祀、踏青等习俗则主要来源于寒食节和上巳节。清明节期间，天气暖和，绿树吐芽，到处都是一片生机勃勃的景象。此时远足踏青，有益于身心健康。宋周密《武林旧事》所载："清明前后十日，城中仕女艳妆饰，金翠深缛，接踵联肩，翩翩游赏，画船箫鼓，终日不绝。"可见宋代时踏青之风已经盛行。清明节的活动几乎是所有春季节日的综合，也具有了更加丰富的文化内涵。

In conclusion, the Qingming Festival is one of the most important traditional festivals in China. Not only is it a festival to honor and commemorate the ancestors, it is also a link for the Chinese people to look for their ancestors and return to their roots. And it is even more a springtime ceremony for going outside, embracing nature and producing new life. Different from other traditional festivals, the Qingming Festival is a combination of a solar term and a custom. The important practices during the Qingming Festival such as sacrificial rites, family outings and so on originated mainly from the Hanshi Festival and Shangsi Festival. During the Qingming Festival, it is becoming warmer, trees are budding, Mother Nature presents lively scenery. It is a good time to go on an outing which is good for both body and mind. As recorded in *Wulin Jiushi* by Zhou Mi of the Song Dynasty, "During the ten days around the Qingming Festival, those leisurely women from official families, richly attired and heavily made-up, would go out shoulder by shoulder, heal after heal to enjoy the beautiful scenery. The entertainment activities featuring gaily-painted pleasure-boats and all kinds of musical performances never ceased day and night." We can see that the practice of hiking was already very popular during the Song Dynasty. In fact, the Qingming Festival is actually the integration of all the springtime holidays and therefore has even richer cultural connotations.

第二章 流布

人生天地之间，若白驹之过隙。从盛唐时期的"上巳曲江滨，喧于市朝路。相寻不见者，此地皆相逢"到宋代的"莫辞盏酒十分劝，只恐风花一片红；况是清明好天气，不妨游衍莫忘归"，上千年时光，弹指一挥间。在时间长河中，上巳、寒食、清明、节气等内容逐渐融合在一起，并且从发源地——华中慢慢地向边疆传播，甚至随着下南洋的华人们远至新加坡、马来西亚、北美等地。清明祭祀和庆祝活动给这些海外游子们带去了慰藉和祝福。

Chapter Two
Dissemination

Man's life in this world is as brief as a glimpse of a white colt flashing past a chink in a wall. From the flourishing Tang Dynasty to the Song Dynasty, a thousand years passed in the twinkling of an eye. A lot of famous poems about the Shangsi and Qingming Festivals have been handed down to date. For example, *Shangsi Ri* by the Tang poet Liu Jia goes, "On the day of Shangsi the banks of Qujiang River are even more bustling than the market. You can meet people there you tried so hard in vain to find". *Jiaoxing Jishi* by the Song scholar Cheng Hao reads, "Don't be unworthy of my sincerity of urging you to drink this glass of wine. Fallen red blossoms will soon lie in profusion. And moreover, today happens to be Qingming, the weather is fine. You'd better go for an outing but never forget to return."

In the long span of time, Shangsi, Hanshi, Qingming as well as solar terms have been mixed together and spread gradually from the place of origin—Central China to the frontier, even to places as far away as Singapore, Malaysia, North America and so on with the overseas Chinese wandering to southeast Asia. The Qingming sacrificial ceremony and celebration activities have brought comfort and blessings to those overseas Chinese.

Chapter Two
Dissemination

1 大 陆
Mainland China

"All over the Spring City (Chang'an) flying flowers everywhere, On Hanshi the east wind blew the imperial willows slant. At dusk within the Han Palace candles are given out, First towards the mansions of the Five Great Lords, the light smoke of the tapers flowed." This is the poem entitled *Hanshi* by Han Hong, the Tang Dynasty poet, which presents an impressive picture of the charming festival. In the story of the origin of the Cold Food Festival, Jie Zitui, the hero was from Shanxi Province, so the practice of cold food was first popular within Shanxi Province and later spread to other places of China. In Shanxi Province, during the Qingming Festival, neither incense nor joss paper were burnt in the southern part at the grave site. The tomb sweepers only hung the spirit money and other accessories at the top of their ancestral graves, hence the saying "a vast expanse of whiteness on

"春城无处不飞花，寒食东风御柳斜。日暮汉宫传蜡烛，轻烟散入五侯家。"唐代诗人韩翃的一首《寒食》，道不尽岁时节令的风流画卷。在寒食节的起源故事中，主人公介子推是山西人，所以冷食习俗首先在山西境内流行，后来才流传到其他地方。在山西，清明节的时候，南部地区上坟不烧香、不化纸，只是将冥钱等物悬挂坟头，有"清明坟头一片白"的说法。但是北部地区要将纸钱香烛等烧尽方可。大同等地的习惯是白天去扫墓上坟，

第二章 流布

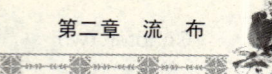

晚上回到家里，再烧化纸钱等。河曲等地的群众，上坟时将祭品带到坟墓前供奉一阵子后，大家在坟前分食酒肴，表示与先祖们共饮共食。闻喜等地，用嵌枣糕在坟堆上滚来滚去表示为亡者挠痒。介休等地，在坟前供上形如盘蛇的面饼，祭毕祖先后，将面饼带回家，晒干后再食用，据说有治病的神效。扫墓祭祖之后，南部地区的人们要拔些麦苗带回家，并且将松枝柏叶或柳条插在门上以辟邪（由桃枝避鬼而来）。北部地区的人们一般只插柳条在门上。东南地区，人人头上插柳枝枯叶，妇女要用描金彩胜(头饰)贴在两鬓。有一些地方也在坟上也插一些柳条。还要制作"红花紫子"为避鬼物，内门缀葫芦悬挂彩纸（葫芦为道家神物，谓能装鬼），挂布袋（装鬼），挂小人手持刀剑、小扫帚，贴五雷符（均是鬼惧怕之物）等，是因为传说清明及清明前后两天为鬼日。

the grave mound during Qingming". However, in the northern region paper money and joss sticks had to be burnt up. In places like Datong City, tomb tending took place during the day and paper money was burnt at night when back at home. The masses in places like Hequ, would bring sacrifices to the front of the grave when visiting their ancestral tombs. After quite a while, all the celebrants would consume wine and other delicacies together before the tomb, an indication of sharing sacrifice with their ancestors. In places like Wenxi, people would roll over some jujube cakes on the tomb mounds, a symbol of scratching the back of the dead. In Jiexiu and other places, cakes in the shape of a coiled snake would be offered in front of the tomb. After the completion of the ancestral worship, the cakes would be brought back home and eaten when dried, which is said to be magic in curing diseases. After sweeping the grave, people in the southern regions would pull some wheat seedlings and take them back home. They would also insert pine twigs, cypress leaves or wickers on the door to ward off evils (from the saying that peach branches can keep off ghosts). People in the northern areas generally inserted wickers on the doors while in the southeast, everyone plugged withered willow branches on the head and women used some gold-coated headdress attached to their temples. In some places, wickers were plugged into the grave. In addition, people would make some ghost-repelling objects called *Honghua Zizi*. The interior doors were decorated with gourds and hanging colored paper (Gourds are Taoism fetish and said to be able to hold

Chapter Two
Dissemination

ghosts), hanging bags (to hold ghost) and puppets armed with swords, brooms and Wulei Fu, literally 5-thunder talisman (all of them are what ghosts fear) and so on, because legend has it that Qingming and the two days before and after it are called Ghost Days.

The traditional sacrificial rites in many northern regions of China include generation offerings, household offerings, making vows to the ancestors and redeem them, etc. Because it is still cold in March in northern China, people will use colorful paper in place of flowers inserted into the grave mound, a symbol of prosperity of the future generations. The mother-in-law would bring her newly-wed daughter-in-law to visit their ancestral grave to pray for their blessings in the hope of getting a lovely boy soon. Once a son was born, the vow must be paid on Qingming the next year. However, you don't have to keep an oath if a girl

北方众多地区的传统仪式包括辈祭、户祭、许愿还愿等。因为北方三月天气尚寒，人们便用五颜六色的彩纸代替鲜花插在坟头，象征后代兴旺发达。婆婆带着新媳妇在祖坟上求祖先赐福，希望早生贵子。一旦生子，次年清明还愿；生女则不必还愿。河北省各地农村，每年夏历三月三，人们挖曲儿菜来吃。提起这一习俗

第二章 流布

的来历，有个曲折神奇的故事。

　　从前有一户人家，就母子俩，儿子盼福上山打柴养活母亲，日子过得很清苦。一天，盼福上山打柴路过山神庙时，见一只大山猫正咬一条小黄蛇，就奔过去把大山猫轰跑了，小黄蛇得救，钻进庙里的一条石缝里。第二天，他在山神庙门口，又见那条小黄蛇趴在那里，挡住了他的去路。盼福绕开小黄蛇，小黄蛇还去拦挡他，盼福就对小黄蛇说："小黄蛇呀小黄蛇，我昨天救了你，你为啥总挡着我的道儿？快放我过去吧。"小黄蛇还是不肯离开。盼福又问："小黄蛇，难道你有啥为难事儿需要我帮助吗？"小黄蛇点点头，转身钻进那条石缝里。盼福跟过去，只见石缝内闪着金光，用手一掏，原来是一块金砖。盼福把金砖交给了庙里的长

was brought into the world. Throughout the rural areas in Hebei Province, people would dig a certain wild vegetable named Qu'er Cai to eat on the third day of the third lunar month every year. There is a magical story full of twists and turns about the origin of this practice as below:

　　Legend has it that once upon a time, there lived a mother and her son named Pan Fu. Every day, Pan Fu went to the mountains to cut woods to feed his mother. Their life was very impoverished. One day, Pan Fu saw a lynx biting a small yellow snake when he passed by a Mountain God Temple on his way to the mountains cutting firewood. He rushed there and drove the lynx away. The small yellow snake was saved and wormed its way into a crevice of a stone in the temple. The next day, at the doorway of the Mountain God Temple, he saw again that small yellow snake lying there, blocking his way. Pan Fu tried to bypass the small yellow snake, but it still blocked his way. So Pan Fu said, "Little yellow snake! Little yellow snake! Yesterday I saved you, why do you keep blocking my way? Please let me go!" The little yellow snake still won't leave. Pan Fu asked again, "Little yellow snake, are you in trouble and need me to help you out?" The little yellow snake nodded, turned around and slipped into the crevice of the stone. Following the snake, Pan Fu saw all of a sudden golden flashes shining in the crevice. Putting his hand in, Pan Fu took out a piece of gold brick. He gave it to the elder of the Temple who gave him 50 taels of silver in return with gratitude.

Chapter Two
Dissemination

Pan Fu spent the 50 taels of silver buying a few acres of land, building a three-room house and also taking a virtuous and beautiful wife. The three-people family were living a better and better life by hard work. Later, Pan Fu hired a painter to draw a picture for his mother, wife and himself respectively and hung all of them on the wall. One day in the early morning, no sooner had Pan Fu opened the window than a gust of whirlwind blew in all of a sudden and swept away the portrait of his wife. At this time, the emperor was choosing at the court his future empress among the captured common girls, none of whom pleased him at all. Suddenly, a gust of wind blew a portrait of a beauty into the court. At the sight of the picture, the emperor glowed with joy immediately. He then ordered his ministers to get in a painter who is asked to draw many copies modeling after the picture and go everywhere to find this woman for him. That day, a few officers and men broke into Pan Fu's house. When they found Pan Fu's wife exactly like the beauty on the picture, they read the emperor's edict about the queen selection. Pan Fu's wife said, "I am a married woman, how can it be?" Pan Fu's mother also pleaded pitifully, "This is my daughter-in-law, please spare her!" A military attache said ferociously: "His Majesty's decree, violators must die!" Pan Fu's wife talked her mother-in-law round and told the military attache, "All right then. But I must see my husband in the field before I go with you." The military

老，长老感激地送盼福五十两银子。

盼福用五十两银子置了几亩地，盖了三间房，还娶了一个贤良美貌的媳妇，一家三口，辛勤耕种，日子越过越好。后来，盼福请一位画匠为母亲、妻子和他自己各画了一幅像，都挂在墙上。一天清晨，盼福刚打开窗子，"呼"地刮来一阵旋风，卷走了妻子的画像。这时，皇上正在宫内选娘娘呢，抓来的民女他一个也不中意。突然一阵狂风刮来一幅美女画像，皇上看了立刻眉开眼笑，吩咐大臣找画师来照样子画了许多张，到各地去寻找这个女子。这天，盼福家闯进几个官兵，他们见盼福的妻子长得跟画像上的女子一模一样，就把皇上选娘娘的圣旨读了。盼福的妻子说："民女是有夫之妇，这怎么行啊？"盼福的母亲苦苦哀求说："这是我的儿媳妇，求你们饶了她吧！"一个武官恶狠狠地说："皇上旨意，违者斩！"盼福

第二章 流布

的妻子劝住母亲，然后对那武官说："好吧，我可以进宫，但必须到地里和我丈夫见上一面。"那武官说："速去速回！"盼福的妻子来到地里，把祸事一说，急得盼福直哭，非要跟官兵拼命不可。妻子拦住他说："盼福，为妻倒有个法子……"她如此这般地说完，又嘱咐一番便含泪走了。盼福按照妻子说的，买了一副弓箭，天天进山打猎，然后用各种兽皮做了顶"百兽帽"，缝了件"百兽衣"，夏历三月初三起了大早，到地里挖了一篮子曲儿菜，戴上百兽帽，穿上百兽衣进了京城。再说皇上逼盼福的妻子成亲，她宁死不从，终日哭哭啼啼。夏历三月初三晚上，从宫外传来"卖曲儿菜"的喊声，她立即转忧为喜，忙唤宫女叫来皇上，说："万岁，民女从小就喜欢吃曲儿菜，现在宫外正有卖的，能不能给我买点儿？"皇上依了，就让宫女买了来。宫女说："那卖曲儿菜的真怪，头戴皮

attache said, "Be quick!" So Pan Fu's wife went to the field and told her husband what had happened. Pan Fu got so furious that he broke into tears and wanted to risk his life. His wife stopped him and said, "Pan Fu, I think I have a way out..." After murmuring her plan in detail to her husband, she enjoined him again and then left tearfully. Following what his wife told him, Pan Fu bought a pair of bow and arrow and went to the mountains hunting every day. Then he made a hundred-animal cap and sew a hundred-animal robe with a variety of animal hides. On the third day of the third lunar month, he got up very early. He went to the field and dug a basket of Qu'er Cai. Putting on the hundred-animal cap and the hundred-animal robe, he left for the capital city. Here in the palace, the emperor forced Pan Fu's wife to get married to him, but she would rather die than obey and keep crying day and night. On the third night of the third lunar month, hearing the cry of "Qu'er Cai on sale" from outside the palace, she beamed with joy immediately. She called her maid to get in the emperor and said, "Your Majesty, I have been fond of eating Qu'er Cai since the childhood. Now it is available outside. Would you please do me a great favor to let me have some?" The emperor agreed and ordered the maid to buy some. Coming back from outside, the maid said, "The seller looks really strange. He wore a hat and a robe with fur outwards, just like a monster." Pan Fu's wife knew in her heart that the seller must be her husband but put on a surprised look on purpose saying, "Can you imagine, Your Majesty, there even exist monster-like

Chapter Two
Dissemination

people? Why not summon him here to have a look?" The emperor nodded in agreement again. When the Qu'er Cai seller was brought into the palace, Pan Fu's wife cannot help giggling. Astounded but highly delighted, the emperor asked, "My dear empress, you have been wearing a worried frown all the time since you entered the palace. Why are you so joyful today?" Pan Fu's wife replied, "Your Majesty, I think his fur hat and robe are really rare, therefore very amusing." The emperor said happily, "If so, I'd like to put them on to please my queen even more." Pan Fu's wife nodded her head, smiling. The emperor, wearing a smiling face, was busy with taking off his crown and dragon robe while ordering the Qu'er Cai seller to take off his fur hat and robe to let him put on. Pan Fu put on the emperor's crown and dragon robe, squeezed some Qu'er Cai into the emperor's mouth, and covered the emperor's head with his basket. At this time, Pan Fu's wife cried out loudly, "Help here! Take this monster out to be beheaded in no time!" From the outside several guards broke in and pushed the emperor out and beheaded him.

帽、身穿皮衣，毛还朝外哩，像个怪物。"盼福的妻子心里明白，装出惊讶的样子说："哦？竟有像怪物的人？万岁，何不把他唤来看上一看？"皇上又依了。当把卖曲儿菜的人带进宫来时，盼福的妻子不禁"咯咯"地笑起来，皇上又惊又喜，忙问："娘娘自进宫以来，总是愁眉不展，今日为何这般欢喜？"盼福的妻子说："万岁，我看他那皮帽、皮衣稀奇，觉得可乐。"皇上高兴地说："如此说来，我要穿戴上，娘娘更会欢喜。"盼福的妻子笑着点点头，皇上笑着忙一面摘下王冠、脱下龙袍，一面命卖曲儿菜的人摘下皮帽、脱下皮衣，他自己穿戴上。盼福穿上皇上的龙袍、戴上王冠，然后用曲儿菜塞进皇上的嘴里，又用篮子扣在皇上的头上。这时，盼福的妻子喊了一声："来人哪，快把这个怪物推出午门斩首。"从门外闯进几

第二章 流 布

个武士，把皇上推出去杀了。

从此，盼福当了皇上，接来了老母，在妻子的辅佐下，把国家治理得很富强，深得百姓们拥护。人们得知是曲儿菜挽救了盼福一家，便认为吃曲儿菜能苦尽甜来，于是每到三月初三这天，都要挖曲儿菜吃，这种风俗便流传了下来。

华中地区的河南省，民间均祭拜和纪念介子推，禁烟火，吃冷食。在湛阳等地，家家多折柳插于门额上，偃师"清明前一日寒食，治酒肴祭墓，剪纸钱挂树"，"士人祭始祖、拜先师、拜先生"。邓州"清明前二日寒日，民间祭扫坟墓，添土，挂纸于颠"。时至今日的商州大荆镇，依然每年都要举办传统的清明会，是因为这样一个传说：

春秋战国时吴、越两国交战，越国战败，越王勾践为保性命把妻妾献给吴王，三太子和母亲趁乱逃出，经过几个月的长途

From then on, Pan Fu succeeded in being the emperor and welcomed his mother to his palace. With the aid of his wife, the country became rich and strong under his governance and he got the full support from his people as a result. Hearing that it was Qu'er Cai that saved Pan Fu's family, people thought that eating Qu'er Cai can turn misery into happiness. Therefore, every year on the third day of the third lunar month, people would dig Qu'er Cai to eat, which is passed down as a custom.

In Henan Province in central China, it is customary to prohibit fire and eat cold food to worship and commemorate Jie Zitui. In places like Zhanyang, willow branches are put on the door to every household. In Yanshi, "On the day right before Qingming, people would eat cold food, prepare food and wine for tomb tending, and cut paper money and hang them on trees", "Intellectuals offer sacrifices to their ancestors, pay respect to Confucius and their own masters". In Dengzhou, "During the two days prior to Qingming, it is a popular practice to sweep the tombs, add new soil and hang joss paper on top of the grave." In today's Dajingzhen, Shangzhou, the traditional Qingming assembly is still held every year because of a legend as follows.

In the Spring and Autumn period and the Warring States period, two coastal states—Wu (in modern-day Jiangsu Province) and Yue (in modern-day Zhejiang Province), were at war and Yue was defeated. For the sake of his own life, King Goujian

Chapter Two
Dissemination

of Yue presented his wife and concubines to King of Wu. Fortunately, the third prince and his mother escaped in disarray. After a few months' long-distance wandering, they came to Dajing, a desolate and sparsely populated place characterized by honest folkways. They settled down here and guided the local people to reclaim wastelands and dredge waterways. After several years' effort, they made people there live and work in peace and contentment. Unexpectedly, during the Qingming Festival one year, at the northwest corner close to Dongyu popped out a mount all of a sudden which kept rising upwards. Everyone was stupefied except the third prince's mother who rushed to the hill without any hesitation. She sat on top of the hill and finally suppressed its increase. At this time, another strange peak emerged which grew even faster. Seeing this, the third prince threw himself towards that peak too. Later, everything came back to normal but both the mother and the son died. Because this happened on Qingming, the locals named the mountain as Mount Qingming. A Goddess Temple and Wuliang Shizu (literally Immeasurable Ancestor) Temple were also built to commemorate the mother and son. Since then, during the Qingming Festival every year, the local people would give opera performances and hold traditional festivities to express their gratitude and respect to the third prince and his mother. Later some commercial activities were added and people from other places went to a fair to trade goods.

跋涉，来到大荆这个土地荒凉、人烟稀少、民风淳朴的地方，母子俩就在这里安家落户，带领当地百姓开垦荒地，疏通水道。经过几年的努力，大家过上了安居乐业的好日子。不料，有一年的清明节，靠近东峪的西北角突然冒出一座山峰，而且不停地向上长。人们都被吓呆了，三太子的母亲义无反顾地扑上去，坐在峰顶上，才将它压住。这时，又一座奇峰冒出来，长得更快。三太子见此情景，也扑向那个奇峰。之后一切都恢复了正常，三太子母子却为此献出了自己的生命。因为这件事情发生在清明节那天，当地人就把此山命名为"清明山"，还在山上修建了娘娘庙和无量始祖庙，以纪念三太子母子。从此以后，每年清明节，当地人都要给三太子母子唱戏、耍社火，以表示对他们的感激和敬意，后来渐渐增加了商

第二章 流布

业活动，外地人都来这里赶会、卖东西。

现在，当地群众每年都要举办大荆清明会，节日活动包括踩高跷、扭秧歌、耍大头娃，十分热闹。就像宋代诗人程颢在《郊行即事》中描述的那样热闹："芳草绿野恣行事，春入遥山碧四周；兴逐乱红穿柳巷，困因流水坐苔矶；莫辞盏酒十分劝，只恐风花一片红；况是清明好天气，不妨游衍莫忘归。"此外，河南还有很多与清明相关的农谚，例如"清明晴，好秧坪"，"清明时节，栽瓜种豆"。

Now, the local people will hold the Dajing Qingming Carnival every year featuring festive activities such as walking on stilts, dancing Yangko, literally "Rice Sprout Song"—a form of Chinese folk dance originating from the Song Dynasty and "big-headed kids" performance, which is as lively as described in *Jiaoxing Jishi* by the Song Dynasty poet Cheng Hao—"Having fun heartily in the green fields. Spring's colour has arrived at the distant mountains. Chasing after the falling blossoms in high spirits through the willow alleys. Sitting on the mossy stones for rest by the river when sleepy." In addition, there are many Qingming-related agricultural proverbs, for example, "Sunny Qingming is good for planting seedlings" and "During Qingming period, plant melons and grow beans".

Chapter Two
Dissemination

The Legend of Zi Fu

In the rural area of the southern part of Shanxi Province, a certain kind of flour food called Zi Fu is steamed in every household during the Qingming Festival every year. Insert an egg (or a walnut) in the middle of a big steamed bun, then knead flour into small animals such as snakes, scorpions, centipedes, geckos and toads to circle the egg (or the walnut), and then fully steam them on some steamer. On the tomb-visiting day, Zi Fu is one of the main offerings for the ritual. After the sacrificial rites, Zi Fu was cut into several equal shares and each family member got one share. It is said that people who ate Zi Fu would be protected and blessed.

Jie Zitui died beside a large willow tree with his mother on his back. He was burnt all over but his face. It is said that the snake, scorpion, centipede, gecko, frog and other small animals covered his face and kept it intact. Hearing the death of Jie Zitui, Duke Wen of Jin beat his breast and stamped his feet in uttermost distress. Then he renamed the mountain Jieshan Mountain and the county where the mountain is located the Jiexiu County. Also he designed the day (right before Qingming) when the mountain was burnt the Hanshi Festival. From that day on, he banned his people to cook food with fire for three days. So when Qingming approaches every year, people would make steamed buns in advance. In addition, to commemorate Jie Zitui, the loyal

"子福"传说

山西晋南一带农村，每年清明节，家家都要蒸一种叫"子福"的面食：在一个很大的馍中间插一只鸡蛋(或核桃)，然后用面捏出蛇、蝎、蜈蚣、壁虎、蟾蜍等小动物的造型，绕在鸡蛋(或核桃)周围，上笼屉蒸熟。上坟那天，子福是祭祀的主要供品之一。祭过祖先之后，子福被切成若干等份，全家每人一份。据说吃了子福会得到祖先的保佑，有福气。

介子推背着老母死在一棵大柳树边。当时介子推只有脸部没有烧焦，据说是因为蛇、蝎、蜈蚣、壁虎、蛤蟆等小动物覆在上面，用自己的身体保住了介子推的面容。晋文公得知介子推的死讯后，捶胸顿足，悲痛至极。他下令把绵山改名为"介山"，绵山所在的县名改为"介休县"，并把放火烧山的那天(清明前一天)定为寒食节。从这天起的三天之内不许生火做饭。

第二章 流布

所以每当临近清明，老百姓便提前把馍馍蒸下。为了纪念介子推这位忠臣，百姓们又在馍馍上捏出蛇、蝎等小动物的图案，并把这种馍馍称作"子福"，是祝介子推的在天之灵有福。

除了全家的总子福外，家里每个人都还有一个小子福。上面的图案因人而异：老人的是福寿盖，男孩的是蛤蟆盖或鱼儿盖，女孩的是石榴盖或莲花盖，都是用面捏的。带有不同盖子的子福还可以作为清明节期间的礼品，在亲友之间互相赠送。据说也是"子福"名称的由来之一，所谓"子福者，你福也"。

虽说子福吃起来与馍馍没有多大差别，但它是一种精美的艺术品，那上面的小动物被女人们捏得惟妙惟肖：张嘴吐信的面蛇、翘着尾巴的蝎子、多腿的蜈蚣、虎视眈眈的壁虎、憨态可掬的蛤蟆、还有打挺的鱼儿、咧嘴的石榴、盛开的莲花……它们给节日增添了活泼的气

officials, people would knead on a steamed bun the patterns of snakes and scorpions and call this steamed bun Zi Fu to wish the spirit of Jie Zitui in Heaven to be blessed.

In addition to the big Zi Fu for the whole family, each family member also has a small one with different patterns on it. The elderlys' Zi Fu has a longevity cover, boys' the frog cover or fish cover, girls' pomegranate cover or lotus cover—all of them are made of dough. Those Zi Fus with different covers can also be used as Qingming gifts among friends and relatives, which is said to be one of the origins of the name of Zi Fu. The so-called Zi Fu means literally "you (are) blessed".

Though Zi Fu tastes almost the same as the ordinary steamed buns, it is a kind of refined art of work with lifelike animals on them from the hands of skillful women—the flour snake that opens its mouth spitting its tongue, the scorpion with its tail sticking up, the multi-legged centipede, the covetously eying gecko, the charmingly naive-looking toad, the fish that bends backwards, the grinning pomegranate, as well as the blooming lotus. They add the lively atmosphere to the festival and express people's best wishes for a better life.

Chapter Two
Dissemination

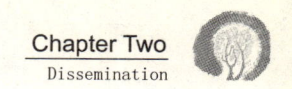

Though the era of Jie Zitui "cut a piece of meat from his own thigh to feed Duke Wen (of Jin)" has passed two thousand years, and the food of the Cold Food Festival is no longer cold, but the folk practice of steaming Zi Fu has been popular ever since.

氛，寄托了人们对美好生活的希望。尽管介子推"割股以啖文公"的时代已过去两千多年，尽管寒食节的食已不再"寒"，但清明蒸子福的民俗却久盛不衰。

第二章 流布

在河北，上坟烧纸钱讲究"早清明，晚十一（农历鬼节）"，也就是说，清明前一周就开始扫墓烧纸了，很少有人选择在清明当天去扫墓祭祖。冀南地区则选择在清明节的前一天的寒食节期间扫墓上坟。陕西宜川县"清明戏秋千、拜坟、做馒头相馈，上缀多样虫鸟，名为子推，谓晋文焚山，禽鸟争救子推也"。但是陕西也有一些地区有提前祭祖的习俗，例如泾阳县就是提前祭祖坟。对于时间的改动，当地有这样一个传说：

当地有一位唱戏的人叫毛旦，清明的时候他回家准备与族人一起祭祖上坟，却被族长拒绝了。毛旦只好在清明节的前两天悄悄在自己父母的坟上添了土，烧了纸，从坟地返回了西安城。毛旦唱旦角，不到二十岁就在省城里唱红了。有一年，新上任的巡抚派人把毛旦请到巡抚府去表演，毛旦回乡时在巡抚

In Hebei Province, in regard to burning paper money, there is a saying of "as early as Qingming, as late as lunar Oct 1st (Lunar Chinese Halloween)", that is to say, tomb sweeping started as early as the week prior to the Qingming Festival and very few people chose to tend the ancestral grave exactly on the day of Qingming. While people in the southern Hebei Province choose to visit the grave site of their deceased beloved the day right before the Qingming Festival. In Yichuan County, Shaanxi Province, "during the Qingming Festival, people play swing, visit the grave sites, and make steamed buns as gifts which are decorated with a variety of birds and insects on the top, called (Jie) Zitui, because it is said that when Duke Wen of Jin had the mountain set on fire, birds contended to save Zitui". However, it is customary in Shaanxi Province to hold ancestor worship in advance, for example, in Jingyang County. About the time changes, there is such a legend as below:

A local opera actor named Mao Dan planned to go back home during the Qingming Festival to visit the ancestral tombs with his clansmen but was rejected by the clan head. Mao Dan could do nothing but add soil to the grave of his parents, burned paper money with nobody's knowledge, and returned from the cemetery to the city of Xi'an two days prior to the Qingming Festival. Mao Dan played the female role and became famous at the provincial capital city when he was not twenty years old yet. One year, the newly appointed governor had Mao Dan invited to his residence to perform. Mao Dan was required

Chapter Two
Dissemination

to return to the capital city before Qingming when he went back to his hometown. The head of *Jia* (In feudal China, a unit of civil administration consisting of 10 households) ordered the whole *Jia* including three villages to celebrate the Qingming Festival and sweep the ancestral tombs two days prior to the Qingming Festival. Since then, the three villages adjacent to Mao Dan's hometown kept the custom of ancestor worship in advance during the Qingming Festival.

There are quite a few agricultural proverbs related to Qingming as a solar term in the oral tradition of the people of Shaanxi Province to highlight its importance. For example, "The rain before Qingming makes the wheat harvest enough for one generation while the rain after Qingming makes the wheat harvest enough for two generations and more" which refers to the influence of the timing of rain to wheat growth. "If the day before Qingming is sunny, no need to sell grain elsewhere"; and "After budding, beans are supposed to be eaten and planted around Qingming". In Shandong Province, willow branches and pine twigs are used to build walls and drive away scorpions. A folk song goes, "One Qingming per year, willow branches are often used to keep off scorpions. During the day they are not allowed to pass by in front of the door and neither can they sting at night."

The sacrificial rites in Jiangsu and Zhejiang Provinces are mainly clan offerings and family offerings, and tomb sweeping and outings are also the main activities. It is customary in the rural

府里许定了返期,不能等到清明节那天。甲头令全甲三个村诸姓一律提前两天过清明祭祖坟。从那以后,毛旦故乡的三个毗邻村庄就留下了清明节提前祭祖的规矩。

作为一个节气,清明在陕西的老百姓的口传中,也有不少相关农谚来说明清明的重要性。例如"清明前有雨兄弟麦,清明后有雨子孙麦",意指降雨的迟早对小麦生长的影响。还有"清明前日晴,菜谷不用寻","出芽,要食旦,种在清明前后"等。山东地区清明节以柳枝和松枝打墙,喝蝎子。民谣云:"一年一个清明,杨柳单打青帮蝎,白天不准门前过,夜里不准把人蜇。"

江浙一带的清明祭祀,以同族祭拜和家祭为主,扫墓踏青亦是主要活动。江浙一带的农村还有

第二章 流布

清明祭蚕神的习俗，道教称蚕神为玄名真人所化，村民感德，立祠奉祭。以顾山为例，位于澄、锡、虞三市（县）交界处的顾山，又称三界山，山顶有庙宇，包括灵官殿、祖师殿和地藏殿等。当地人在清明时举行游顾山的民间拜香活动，集民间信仰、春游、集市贸易、探亲访友于一体，在热闹喧哗中访亲见友。上海清明节的主要活动也是祭扫和踏青，在开辟商埠前，城隍

areas of Jiangsu and Zhejiang Provinces to offer sacrifices to the Silkworm Goddess during the Qingming Festival. Based on Taoism, the Silkworm Goddess is the incarnation of Xuanming Zhenren, literally a mysterious-named enlightened immortal. The villagers felt grateful to the goddess and built a temple to worship her. For example, located at the junction of three cities /counties of Cheng, Xi and Yu, Gushan Mountain is also known as the Sanjie (Three-Boundary) Mountain, on top of which there are some temples including Lingguan Palace, Zushi Palace and Dizang Palace. The locals held the incense burning activity of visiting Gushan Mountain during the Qingming Festival, a combination of folk beliefs, spring outing, fair

Chapter Two
Dissemination

trade and relative-friend visits in a vivid bustling way. The main activities of the Shanghai Qingming Festival are also tomb sweeping and hiking. Before commercial piers were opened up, the City Temple was the only entertainment place for the Shanghai people. On every Tomb Sweeping Day, the locals would carry the City God's statue for a parade, a lively celebration indeed.

On the day right before the Qingming Festival, the county administration notifies the City God in the form of an official document to relieve those nominal and solitary graves on the Tomb Sweeping Day, called the Altar Assembly, also nicknamed Three-Round Assembly because on July 15th and Oct. 1st, the activity was also held. Now when the City God goes on an inspection tour, the Four Departments will follow throughout the city and beyond, but in the earlier times only the guards of honor followed and headed up by the city dwellers carrying flowers. Later young pretty girls of humble birth and prostitutes, richly attired and heavily made-up or putting on chains, participated in the procession sitting in a sedan chair or just on foot, called the female prisoners. So some frivolous young men could not help chasing after and flirting with them. This general mood of society was not forbidden until Ye Tingjuan, the magistrate, had the official banning notice posted during the reign of Emperor Tongzhi of the Qing Dynasty.

In addition to watching the patrol of the Temple God, the Shanghai people also made some seasonal foods for sale and their own eating during the

庙是上海民众唯一的游乐场所，每逢三月清明时，当地人把城隍的塑像抬着出巡，热闹地庆祝一番。

三月清明节前一日，由县移牒城隍神，于清明日到厉台，赈济各义冢及幽孤，名为祭坛会，俗名也叫三巡会，因为七月十五日和十月一日，也要同样举行的缘故。当城隍出巡时，四司每随同遍行城厢内外，早先只有仪仗舆从，士民执香花拥导。后来每有小家碧玉，曲巷烟花，浓妆艳服，披枷带锁，或坐无顶小轿，或竟徒步，参加游行，名为女犯。由是轻薄少年，不免追逐调笑，直到同治年间，知县叶廷眷出示严禁，此风才告禁绝。

除了围观城隍出巡之外，上海的民众还制作一些时令食品，在清明节期

第二章 流布

间出售和食用。青团便是其中之一的点心，由糯米粉制成，经青艾（草头汁）调和而成绿色糕团，中间包上豆沙馅或芝麻馅。食用时并不需要另外蒸煮，而是直接冷食。对上海人而言，青团是清明祭祖时必不可少的供品。

上巳节原本起源于郑国，即今天河南密县与新郑境内，逐渐从郑国流行

Qingming Festival. Qing Tuan (green ball) is one of the snacks made of glutinous rice flour mixed with Qing Ai (green grass juice) with red bean paste or sesame paste as fillings. Cold Qing Tuan is eatable and not necessary to steam. To Shanghai people, Qing Tuan is indispensable in the ancestral worship during the Qingming Festival.

The Shangsi Festival originally stemmed from the State of Zheng, the present-day Mi County and Xinzheng of Henan Province, and gradually spread

Chapter Two
Dissemination

to other places. People along the Xiangjiang River will eat boiled shepherd's purse with eggs on the day of Shangsi. In Changsha and some other places, farmers will listen to the croaks of frogs on this day to predict the harvest, commonly known as "frog report". A local proverb goes, "(If) frogs croak before noon, harvest in highland (rainy); if after noon, lowlands (have) no need to worry (drought)". In places like Changde, it is believed that snakes will get out of their holes on this day, hence the saying "(On)Double-Third Day, snakes out of mountains". People go to the mountains picking Artemisia annua, ground it after cleaning and mix it with glutinous rice flour, and make oblate cakes with sugar or soy bean powder and sugar as fillings, then put them in a steaming utensil, get them out after being ready and eatable, then squeeze them into the holes in the field and the house corners. It is called "collapse of snake eyes", which means blocking snake holes to prevent their coming out to hurt people and livestock. In the southern Huaihua area, a kind of sweet vine cake will be eaten on this day in every household of the Dong ethnic group. And women on this day will be richly attired to cross-stitch flowers basking in the spring wind known as "Flower Cross-Stitching Festival".

In southern Fujian Province far away from the Central Plains, tomb sweeping is not necessarily limited to the Qingming Festival. People in Quanzhou have the habit of Gua Qing, literally "hanging greenery" in front of their ancestral tombs around the Qingming Festival while Zhangzhou dwellers choose to sweep the graves around the

到各地。湘江边的人们，在上巳节这一天，流行吃荠菜煮鸡蛋。长沙等地，老农于这天听蛙声以卜年成，俗称"田鸡报"。当地的谚语常说，"田鸡叫于午时前，丰收在高田(多雨)；叫于午时后，低田不要愁(主旱)"。在常德等地，民间认为此日蛇出洞，俗语云："三月三，蛇出山。"人们进山采摘香蒿，将其洗净磨碎拌上糯米粉，用糖或黄豆粉加糖做心，做成一个个扁圆的粑粑放入甑中，蒸熟后取出，扎紧田坎、屋角的蛇眼，谓之"塌蛇眼"，意即将蛇洞堵住，不让其出山伤人畜。怀化地区南部侗族，这一天家家户户吃甜藤粑，妇女多在这天盛装迎春风挑花，又称"挑花节"。

远离中原的闽南，扫墓的习俗并不一定只在清明期间举行。泉州的人们习惯在清明前后几天到祖坟前挂青；而漳州的人则选择在上巳节前后几天去扫墓；客家人通常选择

第二章 流 布

春节之后去上坟,清理杂草树木,祭拜土地神和祖灵。将"墓纸"用小石头压在坟墓上,表示祭拜完毕。清明节当天不蒸煮食物,以冷食为主。

蜀中的都江堰,人们在清明节时祭拜李冰父子,感谢他们为巴蜀人民带来的风调雨顺。湖北一带的土家族,清明节的时候要制作茅馅儿粑粑,用一种土名叫"茅针"的蒿草,将其嫩芽切碎,去苦水,捣烂后与腊肉丁掺和做成馅儿,再放入糯米团中蒸熟。清明节期间,土家族人民用这些粑粑来祭祀祖先,同时又用它们来待亲接友,互相馈赠。因为这些粑粑是一种避毒蛇的食物,传说,有两条毒蛇成精后危害百姓,有年清明节,玉皇大帝派神仙下凡斩除蛇精。蛇精慌忙隐藏,钻进了磨眼。下凡的神仙顺手拿起一个茅馅粑粑把磨眼盖住。茅馅粑粑有一种刺激味,蛇闻到了就避开。这样,两条

Shangsi Festival. And Hakkas usually prefer to visit their ancestral tombs after the Chinese New Year, cleaning up weeds and trees, worshipping the Earthly God and ancestral spirits. They would put the tomb paper around the tomb with small pebbles on it, an indication of the completion of the sacrificial rites. On the day of Qingming, people would not cook but mainly eat cold food instead.

In the vicinity of Dujiangyan, an irrigation infrastructure, built in 256 B.C. during the Warring States Period, the local people would worship Li Bing and his son during the Qingming Festival to express their sincere thanks for the favorable weather they brought to them. The Tujia ethnic people in Hubei Province would make a certain kind of cake called Maoxian Baba during the Qingming Festival. To make the cake, people would mince the wormwood (its local name being Mao Zhen) shoots, get rid of its bitter water, smash it and mix it with bacon cubes as fillings, and then put them into the glutinous rice ball for steaming. During the Qingming Festival, the Tujia people would use these cakes to make offerings to their ancestors. At the same time they also use them to treat friends and relatives because it is a kind of viper-repelling food. Legend has it that two poisonous snakes endangered people after becoming snake spirits. One year during the Qingming Festival, the Jade Emperor sent immortals to descend to the world to get rid of the snake spirits. In a haste to hide, they slipped into a mill hole. The descending immortals picked up a Maoxian Baba simultaneously to cover the mill hole

Chapter Two
Dissemination

because it has a pungent smell to keep off snakes. As a result, the two snake spirits can never get out any longer. Since then, the Tujias will cover mill holes with Maoxian Baba to prevent snake bites during the Qingming Festival each year.

Similar to the Tujia nationality, there is also a myth among the Zhuang ethnic group as follows:

Legend has it that there lived a childless widow in the Shimen Village, Tanghong Township, Shanglin County, Guangxi Zhuang Autonomous Region. One day, she went to carry water from the pond (locally known as "Shinan Sea") not far from her home. Unexpectedly, after lifting the two buckets, she found a small snake in one of them, she dumped it out. She re-scooped it several times, but each time this snake ran back to the bucket. The widow could do nothing but say: "Since you and I are so destined, I'll take you as my son." In this way, this small snake and the widow became mother and son. It turned out that this snake was not ordinary but a divine dragon in Heaven which lost its magical power and fell into the pond during its pleasure trips. Under the care of the widow, the divine dragon recovered its magic power increasingly, but refused to leave. Whenever floods came, the dragon will sneak into the pool, opening up its scales to capture countless fishes and shrimps. Usually when the widow chopped vegetables to feed pigs, some leaves will fall to the ground, the dragon will use its tail to sweep the leaves back to the basket. Once, the

毒蛇精再也出不来了。从此，恩施人为了防蛇咬，就在每年的清明节期间用茅馅儿粑粑盖磨眼。

和土家族相似的是，在广西壮族群众中，也有一个关于清明节的神话传说：

传说在广西上林县塘红乡石门村有一个寡妇，无儿无女。有一天，她到门前不远处的水塘（当地人称"石南海"）里挑水，把水桶提起来后她发现里面竟然有一条小蛇，于是她就把这条小蛇倒掉了。她重新舀了几次，每次这条小蛇都跑到水桶里去。寡妇无奈地说："既然你我这么有缘，那我就收你做我的儿子吧。"这条小蛇和寡妇就这样成了母子。殊不知，这蛇来历不一般，它本是天上的神龙，由于出来游玩缺失了法力而掉落在水塘里。神龙在寡妇的照顾下法力日益恢复，但它不肯离去，每到洪水来临，神龙就会潜入水潭之中，张开鳞片，捕获鱼虾无数。平

第二章 流布

常，寡妇切菜喂猪，有一些菜叶会掉落在地上，神龙就会用尾巴把菜叶扫回簸箕里。有一次，寡妇不小心把神龙的尾巴砍断了，寡妇好不伤心。从此，大家给神龙取了个壮族的名字，叫作"特掘"。"特掘"翻译成汉语意思就是没有了尾巴的雄性的蛇。后来，寡妇年老得病去世。因为寡妇平时贫困而且小气，大家都不愿意来帮忙下葬。他们对特掘说："你母亲那么疼你，你自己看着办吧。"当时正值清明时节，那夜，风雨交加，闪电轰鸣，特掘盘在搭起蚊帐的竹竿上，眼泪纵横，不一会，窗户被风吹开，一口黑色的棺材飞进屋内，一股清风把寡妇移入棺内。此时，特掘化作飞龙腾空而起，尾随棺材沿着山脊破空而去，山上草石树木纷纷让路，终于，特掘把它的母亲安葬在一个叫"敢仙"的石洞里，并且用河里的泥浆封住棺木。至今，泥浆仍在，里面河蚌、螺蛳、鱼虾残壳

widow accidentally cut off the tail of the dragon, she felt extremely bitter. Since then, people called the dragon Te Jue, a name of the Zhuang Nationality. Translated into Chinese, Te Jue means a male snake that lost its tail. Finally, the elderly widow died of disease. Since she was impoverished and stingy, people were reluctant to help with the funeral and said to Te Jue instead, "Your mother loved you so much, you go ahead and do it by yourself." It happened to be the Qingming period. On that windy night, rain was pouring, with thundering and lighting. Te Jue coiled itself around one of the bamboo poles used to put up the mosquito net, tears pouring. The window was blown open shortly, a black coffin flew into the house, and a puff of fresh air moved the widow into the coffin. At this point, Te Jue turned into a dragon flying into the sky, trailing the coffin away along the ridge piercing the sky, the mountain grass, stones and trees gave way in no time. Eventually Te Jue buried his mother in a stone cave called Gan Xian, literally "brave immortals" and sealed the coffin with the river mud. Until now, the mud is still there with the residues of mussels, screws, fish and shrimps well-preserved inside. The local villagers witnessed this scene, bowed down towards the place of Gan Xian one after another. The folk tale of Te Jue, the divine dragon and its mother spread far and wide. Nowadays, in Shimen Village, whenever the Qingming Festival comes, a spell of spring breeze will blow, accompanied by drizzles, and the people will say joyfully, "It is Te Jue who comes back to sweep its mother's tomb." The life-

Chapter Two
Dissemination

giving spring breeze and rain indicates one year's favorable weather, the protection and blessings obtained from Te Jue and its mother.

Huang Shi, a scholar, holds the view in his article entitled *On the Legend of the Dragon* that the tailless dragon is actually the sign of a storm, which is the explanation of the sudden winds and waves in the South during the Tomb Sweeping Festival. Coincidentally, there is also a legend about the traditional festival among the De'ang Ethnic Group in Yunnan Province. De'ang's most ceremonious traditional festival is Flower Watering Water, also known as Sha Gan Festival or Water Splashing Festival, which is held on the seventh day after the Qingming Festival every year and last three days.

In the early morning of the seventh day after the Qingming Festival , people will put on new clothes, ask partners to go together to the mountain picking fragrant flowers which are to be hung at home or given to neighbors, relatives and friends as a gift to express their festive blessings. Subsequently, people in the stockade will go out of their houses, get together and hold the ceremony of Flower Watering

还保存完好。当地村民目睹了这一幕，纷纷望着敢仙的地方叩拜，"龙母"和神龙特掘的故事广为流传。至今，你到石门村，每逢清明时节刮起一阵春风，伴随着细雨，人们就会喜悦地说："特掘回来扫墓了！"春风化雨，预示着一年的风调雨顺和神龙母子对一方的庇佑和福泽。

学者黄石在《关于龙的传说》一文中，认为掘尾龙反为暴风雨的象征，这是对南方清明前后突如其来的风涛的解释。无独有偶，云南的德昂族也有一段关于传统节日的传说。德昂族最隆重的传统节日是"浇花水"，又称为"沙甘节""泼水节"，是在每年农历清明节后第七天举行，节期历时三天。

清明节后第七天的清晨，人们都换上崭新的衣服，结伴邀约到山上采来香花，或插挂于家中，或馈送乡邻亲友，以表达节日的祝福。随后，寨子里的人们走出家门，聚集在一起，举行浇花水仪式。

第二章 流布

由寨子里一位德高望重的老人，手执花枝蘸着清水轻轻地向大家挥洒，表示仪式的开始。而后，寨子里的人们，就将盛有清水的竹筒高擎过头，轮流将水滴到老人手中以表尊老敬长之意，而老人则手捧清水，一一为滴水的人致祝福之辞，为期三天的节日就在这种尊老爱幼的浓厚氛围中宣告开始了。节日期间，人们用早已备好的水桶、竹筒，盛装清水，互相泼洒，抒发洗去灾祸邪气、迎来吉祥平安的欢乐之情。那些信奉佛教的人家，还要用鲜花蘸着山泉水，清洗家中供奉的佛像，用以表达自己恭敬虔诚的礼佛之心。有些青年男女，更借着节日社交活动的开展，寻觅意中人，结下美好姻缘。德昂寨子里，处处洋溢着欢乐的气氛，德昂族人家，户户充盈着祥和的景象。

福建东部霞浦县一带的畲家人，每年清明后，还有吃春菊糍的习俗。说起这习俗的来历，还有个神奇的传说。

Water. A venerable old man in the stockade will hold a flower branch, dip it in water and gently sway it to everyone, an indication of the beginning of the ceremony. Afterwards, people in the stockade will lift the bamboo tube with water in it over head, take turns to drip water to the hands of the old man to show respect for the aged people. And the old man will hold clear water in his hands and present the speech of blessing to the water-dipping person in return, an announcement of the start of the three-day holiday in the pronounced atmosphere of respecting the elderly and caring for the young. During the holiday season, people will put clean water in the buckets and bamboo tubes already prepared long ago, splash one another to express their joy of washing away evils and ushering in good fortune and peace. The families who believe in Buddhism will also use flowers dipped in mountain spring water to clean up the Buddha statute enshrined at home to express their sincere respect and piety to Buddha. Some young men and women would like to take advantage of the festive social activities looking for the beloved ones to have a good marriage. The entire stockade of De'ang is imbued with the festive atmosphere and all the De'ang households are filled with peace and harmony.

It is customary for the She Ethnic Group in Xiapu County, eastern Fujian Province, to eat a certain kind of cake called Chunju Ci, literally spring chrysanthemum cake after the Qingming Festival every year. Speaking of the origin of this

Chapter Two
Dissemination

custom, there is a magical legend as follows:

A long time ago, there lived on Mount Taimu in eastern Fujian Province a She family consisting of Father and Son. They often did some glutinous rice cakes as snack in the mountains. However, whenever night fell, the cakes were gone. At the beginning, they thought their cakes were stolen but later they found that the thief was not a human being but the scary mandrill. This kind of ashen-faced mandrill does not look like monkeys or dogs. They are so scary, secretive and agile that none of the She family in the mountains dared to provoke it. As a result, the more the mandrill ghost ate, the greedier it became, the more cakes it stole. In the end, the She people had no alternatives but to beg gods for protection. One day, Father brought his son to the Mountain God Temple with a basket of cakes presented to the Mountain God. Suddenly it started to rain heavily and continued for quite a while. The boy felt so hungry that he picked up a cake from the niche and ate it, which his father saw unexpectedly. He stretched out his hand and slapped the cake into the incense burner, saying very angrily, "This is for Bodhisattva, how dare you!" Father then picked up that cake covered with ash and put it back very piously into the niche.

The She people said: "Without piety in worshipping God, three more days needed for a

很早以前，住在闽东太姥山上的一户畲家父子，平时常做一些糍粑，以备进山做点心吃饭。可是，每到晚上，糍粑就不见了。开始，他们还以为是被人偷去了，后来，才发现偷糍粑的不是人，而是可怕的山魈。这种山魈，既不像猴，又不像犬，面部铁青，样子十分可怕，并且来去诡秘，行动迅速，山里的畲家人都不敢去惹它。这样一来，山魈越吃越馋，越馋越偷，畲家人没有办法，只好求神保佑。这天，阿爸提了一篮糍粑，领着阿仔（孩子）来到山神庙供奉山神。忽然天上下起大雨，好久都没停。阿仔肚子饿了，就拿起供龛上的一块糍粑吃。不想被阿爸看见，伸手一掌，把糍粑打落到香炉里。阿爸生气地说："这是敬菩萨的，怎敢乱吃！"接着就拾起这块沾满香灰的糍粑，虔诚地放回供龛。

畲家人说："敬神心不虔，补供得三天。"阿

第二章 流布

爸知道用弄脏的糍粑供神是不虔诚的。第二天，他便带着阿仔再到山神庙补供。到了那里一看，昨天的供品不见了。阿爸说："菩萨真灵！把糍粑都吃了。"阿仔心里不信，东瞧西看，在神龛下找到那块沾有香灰的糍粑。阿爸说："这是菩萨不吃脏了的供品，所以剩下这一块。"阿仔不信，趁阿爸上供品时，又偷抓一把香灰，撒在一块糍粑上。

第三天，父子俩起个大早，去做最后一次补供。阿仔人小步捷，抢先到庙门口，就听到里面有吃东西的声音。他好奇地朝门缝里一望：呀！吃糍粑的不是菩萨，也不是人，是山魈！他就急忙拉着阿爸来看。阿爸一望，吓得蹲在地上，闭上眼睛，祈求山神爷保佑。直等山魈走后，阿爸才走进庙里，匆匆补好供，就带着阿仔回家了。

第四天，阿仔背着阿爸，偷偷来到山神庙，一看，供龛上的干净糍粑都吃光了，留下的又是那块

mending." Father knew that it is impious to offer up dirty sacrifices to God, so the next day, he took his son to the Mountain God Temple to make up for the offering. When they got there, all the offerings from yesterday were all gone. So Father said: "Buddha is indeed the true spirit! He ate up all the cakes." The son didn't believe it in his heart. He looked here and there and found that incense ash-stained cake under the shrine. The father said, "This is because the Buddha does not eat dirty offerings, so this cake was left." The son was still suspicious, so he took advantage of the occasion when his father laid the offerings on the altar to steal a handful ash and sprinkle it on a cake.

On the third day, father and son got up very early to do the last additional offering. Son was small but quick. He arrived at the temple entrance before his father and heard the sound of eating. He was curious to look through the door crevice, "My goodness! It is not the Buddha nor a human being but a mandrill that is eating the cake!" He hastily pulled his father there to have a look. At the sight of the picture, his father was so scared that he squatted on the ground, closed his eyes and prayed for the protection and blessing of the Mountain God. His father didn't walk into the temple until the mandrill was gone. He hastily finished the offering and brought his son back home.

On the fourth day, the son secretly came to the mountain temple without his father's knowledge. He found that all the clean cakes on the niche were gone and what was left was still that incense ash-

Chapter Two
Dissemination

stained cake. In order to solve the riddle, on that night, the son took two rice cakes, rolled them over on the stove ash, and put them together with other cakes on the hanging basket in their house. The next morning, he found that what was left in the hanging basket was none other than that cake stained with stove ash. He was pleased to pick up this cake and eat it, and told his father what he saw in the past two days in detail. The father said, "This is because the ash in the Buddha incense burner can ward off evils, so mandrills did not dare to eat." Unexpectedly, the boy's stomach started to hurt that afternoon. His father said that it was because he was not pious when worshipping god and offended the Buddha, and asked him to eat a handful of ash in the mountain temple incense burner. The boy said that his stomach hurt just because he ate the cake stained with incense ash and refused to eat ash at all. The father could do nothing but pull up a basket of spring chrysanthemum grass which is good for digestion and pain-relief, and use it to make cakes called Chunju Ci together with glutinous rice to feed him.

Strangely enough, since Chunju Ci was made, no mandrills were seen to steal cakes any longer. It turned out that mandrills thought Chunju Ci is moldy because of its furry looks and therefore stopped stealing it. Later, the She people thought that Chunju Ci could ward off demons, evils and diseases, therefore both adults and children love to eat. Since then, the customary practice of eating Chunju Ci after the Qingming Festival was handed

沾有香灰的糍粑。为了揭破这个谜，这天晚上，阿仔又拿两块糍粑滚上灶灰，与其他糍粑一起放在家里的晾篮上。第二天早上一看，晾篮里留下的，果然是那块沾有灶灰的糍粑。他高兴地拿起这糍粑就吃，并将这两天的事一五一十地告诉阿爸。阿爸说："这是菩萨香炉里的香灰能避邪，所以山魈不敢吃。"没想到当天中午，阿仔的肚子痛起来，阿爸说他这是敬神心不虔，被菩萨怪罪了，要他吃一撮山神庙香炉里的香灰来治病。阿仔说自己就是吃了沾有灰的糍粑，肚子才痛的，死活不肯吃。阿爸拗不过他，只好拔来一篮能消积化食又可止痛的春菊草，和粳米一起做成糍粑给他吃。

说也奇怪，自从做成春菊糍后，再也不见山魈来偷糍粑了。原来山魈看到春菊糕那毛茸茸的样子，好像是生了绿霉的，所以就不偷吃了。后来畲家人就认为，春菊糍能防妖避邪、消积去病，大人孩子都爱吃。从此世代沿

第二章 流布

袭下来，形成了清明后吃春菊糍的风俗。

在福建省大田县湖美乡的高峰山下，有个村子叫"林兜"。几百年来，林兜村每年夏历三月初三日，家家户户都要煮"青饭"吃，成了一种风俗习惯。

相传，林姓的祖公叫"十五公"，因被人陷害，关入班房。看守班房的狱卒都是贪吃鬼，凡是犯人家属送进去的食物，都被他们吃了，所以犯人时常饿肚子。十五公也

down from generation to generation.

There is a village called Lin Dou (literally forest pocket) at the foot of Mount High Peak in Humei Township, Datian County, Fujian Province. Over the past centuries, a kind of Green Rice would be cooked in every household on the third day of the third lunar month each year in Lin Dou Village, which became a custom.

Legend has it that the forefather of the Lin family went by Shiwu Gong, literally "15th Man", who got framed and put into jail. All of the prison guards were so gluttonous that they ate up all the foods that the prisoners' families sent into the jail and therefore all the prisoners including Shiwu Gong were often starved. Later, Shiwu Gong's wife, Shiwu Po

Chapter Two
Dissemination

(old woman) came up with a wonderful idea. She collected a certain kind of non-toxic leaves in the mountains, pounded them into pieces in a stone bowl, squeezed them into green juice, added water and rice in the bowl. Soak the mixture overnight, and the rice would be dyed green, then put the rice into the pot and steam, and then the Green Rice is ready. The cooked Green Rice becomes dark green, hence another name Black Rice. On lunar March 3rd, Shiwu Po cooked the Green Rice and brought it to jail. At the sight of the Green Rice which looks like black bat droppings, all of the jail guards could not help pinching their noses and ordered Shiwu Po to bring the food to her husband by herself because they dared not to eat it. From that day on, every day Shiwu Po brought the green food to her husband who no longer got starved ever since. This situation continued until the case came to an end and Shiwu Gong was released from prison.

To commemorate the matter of the Green Rice delivery on March 3rd, the descendants of the Lin family would mark this day as a holiday. On the lunar double third day every year, each and every family must eat Green Rice. In addition, the tree which can produce Green Rice is called Green Rice Tree. When March 3rd was just around the corner, people would begin to invite their relatives, "Please do come over to my home to celebrate the March Festival together." When the relatives left after the March Festival, they would give them a

没吃饱。后来，十五公的老伴十五婆就想了一个巧妙的办法，上山采来一种无毒的树叶，舂碎后，绞出青绿色的叶汁，加水拌米浸泡，浸了一个晚上，米粒就染成青绿色，再放入锅里蒸，就成了青饭。煮熟的青米饭，变成暗绿色，所以也叫"乌饭"。十五婆在三月初三这一天，煮了青饭，送进班房。狱卒见了这黑不溜秋像蝙蝠屎似的青饭，一个个捏着鼻孔，不敢吃，叫十五婆自己送进去给十五公吃。从这一天起，十五婆每天送青饭，十五公就不用饿肚皮了。青饭一直送到案件了结、十五公出班房为止。

林家的子孙为了纪念三月初三送青饭的事，就把这一天当作节日来过，每年农历三月初三，家家户户都要吃青饭，并把这种能做青饭的树叫作"青饭树"。未到三月三，就开始邀亲戚："来我家过'三月节'啊！"过了三月节，亲戚告别回家，还要送一包青饭做盘头。后

第二章 流布

来，邻村长扳、后坪姓吴的人，看见林兜人过三月节真有趣味，青饭又太好吃，也开始吃青饭过三月节，时间一长，就形成了风俗。

居住在云南省澜沧、孟连等自治县的拉祜族，每年三月，采摘、揉吃揉揉果。说起它的来由，还有个古老而神奇的故事。

传说从前有个猎人在老林里撵一只金马鹿。金马鹿跑得飞快，勇敢的猎人从清早追到天黑，终于把金马鹿捕获了。这时，猎人已累得又饥又渴。可是，他身上带着的干粮早吃完了，只有半葫芦水挂在腰间。他拿起葫芦刚要喝，见身旁一棵刚出土的小树苗快枯死了。猎人心想：这半葫芦水喝了也只能解一时之渴，如果浇到了小树苗上，这小树长大了便能活上百把年。于是，他把水浇到小树苗的根上。当猎人浇完水，挂起刀和弓箭，扛起金马鹿

packet of Green Rice as a farewell gift. Later on, the Wu families in the neighboring villages such as Changban and Houping also followed suit. They also ate Green Rice in celebrating the March Festival because they saw a lot of fun in Lin Dou people's celebration and the Green Rice tasted so good! With the lapse of time, this custom came into being.

In the lunar March each year, the Lahu Ethnic Group living in some Autonomous Counties such as Lancang and Menglian in Yunnan Province will pick up a certain kind of fruit which they will rub before eating, hence the name Rubbed Rubbed Fruit. Speaking of its origin, there is an ancient and magical story as follows:

Legend has it that once upon a time, a hunter was chasing a golden Cervus elaphus which ran very fast in the forests. The brave hunter had been running after the golden Cervus elaphus from dawn to dusk and finally captured it. Exhausted, the hunter was very hungry and thirsty. However, all the food on him was gone, only half gourd of water hanging in the waist. He picked up the gourd, about to drink and saw that the newly sprouting small tree nearby was about to be withered. The hunter thought in his mind, "This half gourd of water can only quench my thirst temporarily, but if I sprinkle it into this small sapling, it will live hundreds of years when it grows up. So he watered the root of the sapling. When the hunter finished watering, he hung his knives and arrows on his shoulders, put the golden Cervus elaphus on his back and was going back to the village, he suddenly heard a voice from an sour

Chapter Two
Dissemination

fruit tree beside the small sapling, "Kind-hearted young man, thank you very much for saving my child. You look very hungry and thirsty, please do pluck a couple of fruits from my branches to eat."

Hearing this, the hunter took a look at the sour fruits on the tree, and could not help sucking from his mouth before eating. The sour fruit tree read the mind of the hunter and went on, "Kind-hearted hunter, let me tell you the secret. You rub the fruit in your palms several times, and the fruit will become sweet." Following what the fruit tree told him, the hunter plucked a sour fruit and rubbed it in his palms. Just as expected, the sour fruit tasted as sweet as honey. Since then, the Lahu people have been fond of eating sour fruits. Even today, in March every year on the lunar calendar, the Lahu people will pluck sour fruits and eat them after rubbing, hence the name "Rubbed Rubbed Fruit".

正要回村寨的时候，忽然听见小树苗旁边的一棵酸果树说道："好心的小伙子，谢谢你救了我的孩子。看你又饥又渴，从我树枝上采几个果子吃吧。"

猎人听了，看了看树上的酸果，还没吃便酸得噘起了嘴。酸果树看出了猎人的心思，接着又说："善良的猎人，我把秘密告诉你吧，只要把果子在手掌心里揉几下，果子就能由酸变甜啦！"猎人听了果树的话，便采了一个酸果在手掌心里揉了揉，果然酸果的味道变得像放进了蜜糖一样甜。从此，拉祜族人爱吃酸果子。直到今天，每年夏历三月拉祜族人都把酸果采来揉着吃，所以叫它"揉揉果"。

第二章 流布

2 港台
Hong Kong and Taiwan

清明节是香港人的重要节日。在香港及新界地区，自古以来就有居民祭祀祖先的习俗，尤其以立春、清明、重阳和冬至时期的祭祀为最重要。清明和重阳节时，居民多到山上祭拜祖先。每逢清明时节，香港人带着香纸烛以及水果、鲜花和其他祭品到祖先坟前祭拜。与内地不同的是，香港人往往会提前几天去拜山，以错开人多拥挤的状况。此外，还有深港两地的市民跨境扫墓，香港的一些市民亦会返回百余年前建的宗祠去祭拜祖先。

The Qingming Festival is an important festival to the people in Hong Kong. There has been a custom of ancestral worship since ancient times in Hong Kong and New Territories. The offerings especially in the periods of the beginning of spring, Qingming, Double Ninth Festival (or Chongyang Festival) and the Winter Solstice are the most important. On the Qingming Festival and Chongyang Festival, most of the Hong Kong residents will worship their ancestors in the mountains. During the Qingming Festival, the Hong Kong people will bring joss sticks, candles, fruits, flowers and other sacrifices to their ancestral grave site and worship. Different from Mainland China, the Hong Kong people tend to worship the mountain a few days in advance in order to stagger the crowded condition. In addition, citizens in Shenzhen and Hong Kong will do cross-border tomb sweeping, and some Hong Kong

Chapter Two
Dissemination

residents will also return to their ancestral hall over a hundred years ago to worship their ancestors.

There used to be a Feng Shui saying that "Fire makes the land prosperous" when cleaning up the weeds around their ancestral tombs, but people gradually abandoned this custom in recent years for the sake of safety and prevention from hill fires. Different from Mainland China, Hong Kong citizens are often used to buying a bouquet of flowers and attach it to the gravestone when worshipping their ancestors during the Qingming Festival. Chrysanthemums, carnations, roses and other flowers are the best-selling commodities during the Qingming Festival. This is also the habit into which the people of Hong Kong have developed in recent years, an indication of changes in traditional customs.

The Qingming customs in Taiwan are quite similar to those in southern Fujian Province. In most regions, Qingming falls on around the third day of the third lunar month or the second day of the second lunar month. When visiting the ancestral tombs, people will bring cakes, rice crackers, and other offerings and place them in front of the tombstone, and also trim the weeds and trees around the grave site. After the cleaning is finished, people will put the "tomb paper" (5-colored, rectangular paper cuts) around the grave pressed with stones, then put a stack of the tomb paper on the tombstone. The ceremony is called "hanging paper". After the trimming of the graves is done, the whole family are supposed to eat red eggs around the graves, and scatter the egg shells in the cemetery. They should

以前，上坟清理杂草的时候往往有"火烧旺地"的风水说法，但近年来为了安全和防止山火，市民逐渐放弃了这一习俗。与内地不同的是，香港市民在清明节祭祖时往往习惯买上一束鲜花插在墓碑前。菊花、康乃馨、玫瑰等鲜花都是清明节的畅销商品。这也是香港市民近些年养成的习惯，传统习俗也在发生着变化。

台湾民众的清明习俗，与闽南差不多，时间大多在农历三月初三前后，也有在二月初二的时节。扫墓时，带上糕点、米果等祭品摆放在墓碑前，对坟墓周围的杂草树木进行修整。打扫完毕后，要在坟墓的四周用石头压上"墓纸"（用五色纸剪成长方形），然后放一叠墓纸在墓碑上，这个仪式被称为"挂纸"。修整完坟墓后，全家人要在坟墓四周吃红鸡蛋，蛋壳撒在墓地上。扫墓时，也要祭

第二章 流布

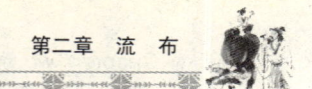

拜土地公，另外要把糕点分发给小孩子们。

also worship the Earthly God and distribute the pastries among small children.

Chapter Two
Dissemination

3 海 外
Overseas Chinese Communities

Southeast Asia has a unique clan culture which is closely related to the traditional ancestral worship of the overseas Chinese during the Qingming Festival. All the Chinese who made a living in Southeast Asia far away from home in the early years pooled money to buy land, built Yishan (free cemetery) and Dabogong (God of Land) Temple in order to achieve the common desire of the ancestral worship. Before 1860, the Qing government strictly prohibited the subjects from emigrating, but in fact male immigrants or coolies still chose to leave for Southeast Asia and then returned home to get married after making enough money. When abroad, in accordance with the traditional customs, they would worship the ancestors in Spring (Qingming Festival) and Autumn (Ghost Festival).

Today in Singapore where the Chinese account for about 75% of the total population, the

东南亚地区拥有独特的宗乡会馆文化，与华侨的清明节祭祖传统密切相关。早年闯荡南洋的华人共同凑钱置地，建义山（免费公墓），盖大伯公（土地神）庙，以实现共同的祭祖愿望。1860年前，清政府严厉禁止臣民移居海外，但是实际上男性移民或苦力依然出发前往南洋，挣钱之后再返回家乡娶亲。他们在海外时，按照传统习俗，于春（清明节）、秋（中元节）两节敬拜祖先。

在华人约占总人口75%的新加坡，新加坡华

第二章 流布

人至今仍按照闽南仪式在清明时节去扫墓。先祭祀土地神，然后在亲人墓前摆上酒食、果品和鲜花，燃起香烛，压上墓纸，再将纸钱焚化，磕头行礼，最后当场将酒食、肉、果吃完回家。祭拜完毕当场剥蛤吃，然后把蛤壳丢在坟前，表示子孙已来扫过墓。有些新加坡华人还会在清明时节返回中国的老家祭拜祖先。

Singaporean Chinese will still sweep the tombs in accordance with the Minnan (Southern Fujian Province) ceremony during the Qingming Festival. They first offer sacrifices to the God of Land, then lay food, wine, fruits and fresh flowers in front of the graves of their beloved deceased, and then light joss sticks, press tomb paper around the tombs, and then incinerate paper money, kowtow and salute, and finally eat up on spot all the food, wine, meat and fruits and go back home. After the worship is completed, they will shell clams to eat on the spot and then throw away the clamshell in front of the graves, an indication that the descendants have already swept the tombs. Some Chinese in Singapore will return home in China to worship their ancestors during the Tomb Sweeping Festival.

Chapter Two
Dissemination

In Malaysia, the main activity during the Qingming Festival is tomb sweeping to show respect for the ancestors. Offerings include Three Animals (cow, sheep and pig), wine, cakes, fruits, flowers, eggs and so on. The Malaysian Chinese will even present a whole golden roast pig as an offering. During the Qingming Festival, some Clan Associations and Fellow-townsman Associations established on kinship and geography respectively will also send people to bring offerings like incenses and candles to the free graveyards to offer sacrifices to those childless fellow-townsmen and members. Ipoh the Sambo Temple in Malaysia is the place for keeping the ashes of the deceased Buddhist. Every year during the Qingming Festival, the family members will present offerings to worship their deceased beloved and pray for their souls.

With the increase of communication between China and Southeast Asian countries, the activities of the Chinese root-seeking and ancestor-visiting are also increasing. During the Qingming Festival in 1999, the five descendants of Jose Rizal (1861—1896), the founding father of the Philippines made a special trip to Guocun Village, Luoshan Township, Jinjiang City, Fujian Province to worship their ancestors. There is also the worship feast called Si Qing in many assembly halls of the Burma Chinese during the Qingming Festival which is usually held exactly on the holiday or before. As in China, it is also customary to enjoy the greenery of springtime and tend to the graves of departed ones in Vietnam during the Qingming Festival when people will tend

在马来西亚，清明节的主要活动是祭祖扫墓。供品有三牲、酒、汀饼、水果、鲜花、桂点、蛋等，马来西亚华人甚至还供上金黄色的整只烤猪。一些以血缘和地域组成的宗亲会和同乡会等社团，在清明节时，还派人携带香烛祭品，前往义冢祭祀那些无子嗣的同乡和会友。马来西亚的怡保三宝庙，是佛教徒死后存放骨灰的场所。每年清明节，亡者家属带来供品祭祀死者，并为亡灵祈祷。

随着中国与东南亚各国交往的增多，华人寻根探祖的活动也越来越多。1999年清明节，菲律宾国父何塞·黎刹家族的五位后人专程到福建省晋江市罗山镇郭村拜祭先人。缅甸华侨的许多会馆清明节时也有"祀清"的宴叙，常在清明正日或提前举行。与中国一样，越南清明节也有扫墓踏青的习俗，人们带着蜡烛、鲜花、水果、香、纸钱等，修理坟墓，纪念祖先。

第二章　流布

韩国非常重视传统的节日，春节和中秋节是最隆重的节日，各自放假三天。另外，端午节、清明节、寒食节虽非公休日，也都有纪念。清明是二十四节气中的第五个，在古代，它的重要性并不如寒食节，扫墓也是后来才有的活动。在宫殿里会燃烧柳枝和榆树枝，再分给各司，来显示火的重要。韩国的寒食节也是沿袭中国的习俗而来的，有时候在三月，有时候在二月，准备水果和糕点等祭品到祖先的坟前举行祭祀活动。寒食节期间不能生火，只能吃事先煮好的食物。

上巳节也传入韩国，又被称为"重三"，民间盛行摘下一些杜鹃花瓣，和面粉做成"花煎"；或是和上绿豆粉，煮熟后涂上蜂蜜切成面条，这就是"花面"，还可以加上其他颜色，用五味子汤水浇上去，再加蜂蜜和松子来

the graves with candles, flowers, fruits, incense as well as paper money to commemorate the ancestors.

Korea attaches great importance to traditional festivals, among which the Spring Festival and the Mid-Autumn Festival are the most formal three-day holidays. In addition, though the Dragon Boat Festival, Qingming Festival, and Cold Food Festival are not the public holidays, they are still observed. Qingming is the fifth of the 24 solar terms. In ancient times, it was not as important as the Cold Food Festival, and tomb sweeping activity was added to the celebration later. The branches of willow and elm trees will be burnt in the palace and then distributed among various divisions to show the importance of fire. The Cold Food Festival in South Korea also followed the Chinese customs. Fruits, pastries and other things are prepared for the worship ceremony in front of the ancestral tombs sometimes held in March and sometimes in February. During the Cold Food Festival people cannot light fire but only eat food cooked in advance.

The Shangsi Festival was also introduced into South Korea, also known as "Double-Third", during which it is popular for people to pluck some rhododendron petals and flour to make a certain kind of food called Hwajeon, "flower cake" in Sino-Korean, or mix rhododendron petals with green bean flour, cook it, mince it, and then coat it with honey, and finally cut it into noodles, called "flower noodles". You can also add other colors to the

Chapter Two
Dissemination

noodles using schisandra soup as gravy, add honey and pine nuts, and then eat. During the Shangsi Festival, women may use butterflies for divination. If the yellow butterfly or tiger-butterfly meets your eyes first, it means that your desire can be achieved; if you see a white butterfly first, it is an ill omen, an indication of the death of your parents. During the period from March 3rd to March 8th, women in Chungcheong bukdo will invite female Koradji to exercise magic for son bearing. Moreover, women will wash their hair on this day in a special way and believe that their hair will be light and supple, therefore charming.

During the Qingming Festival, the South Koreans tend to make a variety of delicate food and drinks. Each family will make their own wine. Wines that are good for spring are azalea wine,

吃。上巳节的时候，妇女可以用蝴蝶来占卜，先看见黄蝴蝶或是虎斑蝴蝶，表示愿望可以实现，先看见白蝴蝶则是凶兆，表示会有父母丧。在三月三日到八日期间，忠清北道地方的妇女会请巫堂（泛指巫女或巫师）作法祈子。此外，妇女会特别在这天洗头，相信头发会轻盈柔顺，丝丝动人。

清明节期间，韩国人往往制作各种精美的食物和酒水。每家还会自己酿酒。适合春天喝的酒有杜

第二章 流布

鹃酒、桃花酒、小面酒、梨花酒、竹沥酒、瑞香酒、四马酒等。这些酒不但有春天的气息,还显现出家风以及主人的风流。有些人家还会将百日酒埋在近大门口旁的地底下,以防被人提早开封喝掉。糕点也是清明节受欢迎的

peach wine, pear wine, Daphne wine and so on. Not only do these wines smell of spring, but also show the family tradition as well as the refinement of the host and hostess. Some families will also bury Hundred-Day Wine under the ground near the main entrance just in case that others unseal it and drink it in advance. Pastries are also popular during the Qingming Festival, among which keikeu cake is most representative. You can make keikeu cake

Chapter Two
Dissemination

with glutinous rice flour, put fillings in the middle, and then knead them into various shapes such as crescent and round, decorated with multiple colors on the top.

食物,其中以"散饼"最具代表性。散饼是用糯米粉做的,中间包馅儿,再捏成各种不同的形状,例如半月状、圆形等,上面再点缀五彩颜色。

第三章 风俗

"梨花风起正清明,游子寻春半出城。日暮笙歌收拾去,万株杨柳属流莺。" 宋代诗人吴惟信的这首《苏堤清明即事》,生动地描绘了宋代清明时节踏青聚会的场景。自先秦时起,清明节的习俗大部分都延续下来,扫墓家祭、踏青、饮食等内容,亦是现代人所践行的习俗。

Chapter Three

Customs

"Peach flowers in the Qingming wind are blossoming.

Half the city went out for an outing.

At dusk, all music and singing faded away.

Only orioles are chirping pleasantly on thousands of willow trees."

This poem entitled *Sudi Qingming Jishi* by Wu Weixin, the Song Dynasty poet, depicts vividly the scene of outings and parties during the Song Dynasty Tomb Sweeping Festival. Since the Pre-Qin period, most of the Qingming customs remained. The tomb sweeping, family offerings, springtime outings and food regulations are also practices of modern times.

Chapter Three
Customs

1 扫墓与祭祖
Tomb Sweeping and Ancestor Worshipping

It was customary to hold sacrificial rituals in spring and autumn, spring offerings took place during the Qingming Festival and autumn offerings during the Chongyang Festival on the ninth day of the ninth month in the Chinese calendar. According to the records in *Yudi Ji*, "Sacrificial rituals: scholar-officials' temple worship, like Duke Wen's familial ceremony, common folks dared not build ancestral halls, the ceremony was mostly simple. The sacrificial ceremony took place at the graveyard during the Qingming Festival and in lunar mid-July; at home or at the tomb site on lunar October 1st; and at home on the winter solstice, at the end of the lunar year and on the death day." That is, the sacrificial rites were divided into two categories-indoor offerings and outdoor offerings. However, before the Qin Dynasty (221 B.C.—206 B.C.), the sacrificial ceremony did not include tomb sweeping

古俗本有春秋祭祀，春祭在清明，秋祭在重阳。根据《舆地记》记载："祭礼：士大夫庙祀，率如文公家礼，民间不敢立祠堂，礼多简朴，清明祭于墓，七月中旬祭于墓，十月一日祭于家，或祭于墓，冬至岁暮忌日，俱祭于家。"即将祭祀礼仪分为家祭和外祭两类，但实际上秦代以前，祭祀都没有扫墓这一项，上坟的习俗源自于汉代。《晋书·礼志》记载："古无墓祭之礼，汉承秦皆有园陵。"唐代，清明扫墓祭祖是主要活动，并

第三章 风 俗

且已经成为官方规定。高宗永徽二年（651年），有司上书，请高宗从太宗祭祀高祖的旧制，于清明寒食时"上食如献陵（高祖李渊陵）"。又据《旧唐书·玄宗纪》，寒食节上墓拜扫，礼经无文，但近代相沿，积久成俗。鉴于此俗已久，唐玄宗于开元二十年（732年）下诏"士庶之家，宜许上墓，编入五礼，永为常式"。自此，清明寒食扫墓用诏令形式正式确定下来，列入五礼之中。唐宋时期，在寒食期间也要扫墓祭祖，如《唐书》记云："开元二十年敕，寒食上墓，《礼经》无文。近代相传，寝以成俗，宜许上墓同拜扫礼。"《岳阳风土记》载："春社后，遇好天色，往往相继上山，州人所谓拜扫也。至寒食而止。"

which originated from the Han Dynasty. *Jin Shu: Li Zhi*, or *The Book of Jin: Rituals Treatises* recorded, "There were no tomb offerings in ancient times, inherited from the Qin Dynasty, there were funerary cemeteries in the Han Dynasty (206 B.C.—220 A.D.)". In the Tang Dynasty (618—907), tomb sweeping and ancestor worship were the main activities during the Qingming Festival and became the official regulations. In 615, some divisions were presented to Emperor Gaozong a memorial asking him to follow the old practice that Emperor Taizong (627—649) visited the Xianling Mausoleum of Emperor Gaozu (618—626) during the Qingming and Hanshi Festivals. Also based on *Jiu Tang Shu: Xuanzong Ji*, or *The Old Book of the Tang Dynasty: Biography of Emperor Xuanzong*, there were no written text in *Li Jing*, or *Book of Rites* for tomb sweeping during the Hanshi Festival, but it gradually developed into a custom in modern days inherited from ancient times. In view of this long-honoured custom, Emperor Xuanzong (712—756) issued an edict in the 20th year (732) of the Kaiyuan era (713–741), "Families of scholars and the common people should be allowed to visit graves to honor their beloved deceased. This should be categorized into the *Wu Li*, or *Five Rituals* (i.e. Ji Li—Good Luck Rituals which refer to all kinds of worships; Xiong Li—Bad Luck Rituals referring to funerals; Jun Li—Military Rituals; Jia Li—Good Rituals referring to the Coming-of-age Ritual and Marriage Ritual, and Bing Li—Guest Rituals, as an eternal routine). Since then, tomb sweeping during the

Chapter Three
Customs

Qingming and Hanshi Festivals has been officially defined in the form of an imperial edict and included in the Five Rites. In the Tang-Song period (618—1279), people would also sweep the ancestral tombs during the Hanshi Festival, as recorded in *Tang Shu*, or *Book of Tang*, "The edict in the 20th year of the Kaiyuan era of Emperor Xuanzong reads—There is no written text regarding tomb sweeping during the Hanshi Festival. However, it is handed down to modern times and has developed into a custom. Therefore, it should be permitted to be regarded as a ritual." *Yueyang Fengtu Ji* also recorded, "After the spring sacrifice, when the weather is good, people would go to the mountains one after another, the so-called tomb sweeping by the locals. It would stop by the Hanshi Festival."

The grave tending practice during the Ming Dynasty (1368—1644), almost exactly the same as today, mainly included burning incense for the dead, laying offerings on the altar, cleaning up weeds and tree branches and setting up tombstones. In the Ming Dynasty, the paper money to be burnt is specially made, also called Guang Ming (bright) or Wangsheng Qian (afterlife money) which ghosts or spirits or the dead are given to use in the nether world. There

明代的扫墓习俗，与当下几乎无二，主要是为死者烧香上供、清除杂草树枝和立碑。明代时焚烧的纸钱是特制的纸钱，又称"光明"、"往生钱"，是送给鬼神或死人在冥世间使用的。另外还有一种"压钱"，即把纸

第三章 风俗

钱压在坟堆的四角、坟顶而得名。清代时，祭祖习俗逐渐丰富，"清明男女簪柳，出扫墓"，"士庶并出，祭祖先坟墓，谓之上坟。间有婿拜外父母墓者……凡娶新妇，必挚以同行，谓之上花坟……家祭、墓祭皆焚化纸锭"。

is also a kind of money which will be pressed around the four corners of the burial mounds or on top of the tomb, hence the name Ya Qian (pressed money). During the Qing Dynasty, the custom of ancestor worship was gradually various, "During the Qingming Festival, men and women would wear a wicker on head and go out for tomb sweeping"; "Both the scholars and the common folks would go out to worship their ancestors at the grave site, called tomb visiting. Occasionally, there were sons-in-law who visited the tomb of their parents-in-law...A newly-wed woman must go together with her husband to worship his ancestors at the tomb, called Shang Hua-fen, literally 'visit a flower tomb'...Paper money would be burnt during both home offerings and tomb offerings".

Chapter Three
Customs

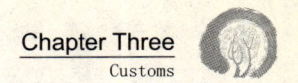

During the Qingming Festival in modern times, the rituals of ancestor worship at home or in the clan ancestral hall remained the same as before—place the altar table in front of the memorial tablets of the ancestors, then put a variety of sacrifices on the table, and then the whole family would burn incense and kowtow before the altar table.

近代的清明时节，家中或宗族祠堂内祭祀祖先的仪式照旧，于祖先牌位前摆上供桌，桌上放置各种祭品，然后家人于供桌前焚香叩拜。

第三章 风 俗

2 踏 青
Go for an Outing in Early Spring

踏青，是清明节的主要活动。在先秦的上巳节和寒食节期间，踏青郊游就是主要内容之一，唐宋时期依然如此。唐玄宗在天宝十三年（754年）与诸宫娥出东门郊游踏青。南宋时期流传的《西湖三塔记》亦是从官宦子弟在清明时节外出踏青所遇到的一系列故事开始：

Going outside and enjoying the greenery of springtime is the main activity during the Qingming Festival. During the Shangsi Festival and Cold Food Festival in the Pre-Qin period, springtime outing was one of the main activities, which remained so in the Tang and Song Dynasties. For example, in 754, Emperor Xuanzong of Tang went out of the East Gate for an outing in the early spring accompanied by his concubines. The story entitled *Xihu Santa Ji,* or *Story of the Three Pagodas on West Lake* popular during the Southern Song Dynasty (1127—1279) also starts from a series of events that those children of officials witnessed on the way of their springtime hiking in the Qingming period.

Chapter Three
Customs

Xi Xuanzan, a young man from an official's family, met a girl in white during his visit of West Lake in the Qingming period and took her back to his home. Later, the girl's grandmother in black came and Mr. Xi walked them home. The girl's mother, a woman in white, treated him with human hearts and had sexual relation with him. After co-habitating for half a month, the woman in white got tired and intended to kill Mr. Xi and gouge out his heart. The girl in white saved him and set him free. The next Qingming, Mr. Xi shot down a crow which turned back into the grandmother in black, so Mr. Xi was once again kept in the house of the woman in white. Again, the girl saved him. This time after he came back home, his uncle, Taoist Xi learned what happened to him and exercised magic to catch the three demons. Later they revealed their true features—the white-clothed woman is a white snake,

一个官宦子弟奚宣赞清明时节游西湖，遇一白衣女孩，带她回了自己家。稍后，女孩的黑衣祖母找来，公子送她们返家。女孩的母亲白衣妇人取人心款待公子，并以身相许。同居半月，白衣妇心生厌倦，欲杀公子取其心。女孩救了他，放他回家。次年清明，奚公子射落乌鸦，乌鸦变回黑衣祖母，奚君又被因于白衣妇人家，女孩再次施救。这次他回家后，他的叔父奚真人得知此事，用道法捉三妖。后其现形，白衣妇为白蛇，女孩为鸡妖，黑

第三章 风俗

衣祖母为獭妖。奚真人化缘，造三石塔，镇三怪于湖中。

据考证，《白蛇传》是从《西湖三塔记》演绎而来。可见，踏青是当时青年男女认识和聚会的重要方式之一。《东京梦华录》亦描述了清明踏青的盛景：

清明节，寻常京师以冬至后一百五日为大寒食。前一日谓之"炊熟"，用面造枣䭅飞燕，柳条串之，插于门楣，谓之"子推燕"。子女及笄者，多以是日上头。寒食第三节，即清明日矣。凡新坟皆用此日拜扫。都城人出郊。禁中前半月发宫人车马朝陵，宗室南班近亲，亦分遣诣诸陵坟享祀，从人皆紫衫白绢三角子青行缠，皆系官给。节日亦禁中出车马，诣奉先寺道者院祀诸宫人坟，莫非金装绀憶，锦额珠帘、

the girl is a chicken demon and the black-attired grandmother is an otter demon. Taoist Xi begged alms, built a three-stone tower and surppressed the three demons in the lake.

According to textual research, *Baishe Zhuan*, or *Legend of the White Snake* comes from *Xihu Santa Ji*. Obviously, springtime outing was one of the important ways in which young men and women got to know one another and got together. Meng Yuanlao in his book *Dongjing Menghua Lu*, or *The Dreams in the Eastern Capital*—a very detailed description of the daily life in the Northern Song Period (960—1127) capital of Kaifeng, Henan Province, also describes the spectacular Qingming outing below:

During the Qingming Festival, usually in the capital city the 105th day after the winter solstice was most important. The day before the Hanshi Festival was called Cooked Day when banners were made out of flour mixed with cooked jujube with a flying swallow design on them, strung together with wickets, and put at the gate or front doors, called (Jie) Zitui Swallow. When girls came of age, that is, reached the age of fifteen, most of them would wear their hair bound up and held in place by a pin on this day. The third day of the Hanshi Festival was the day of Qingming. All new tombs were swept on this day. All the capital dwellers went out to the suburbs. In the imperial palace for the first half of the month, servants and vehicles were sent to visit the mausoleums. The royal clansmen and close relatives were also dispatched to different

Chapter Three
Customs

mausoleums. The retinues were all wearing purple robes, white silk strips and triangular hoods of green sackcloth over their heads, all of which were from the government. Carriages were also sent from the forbidden royal palace to visit the tombs of the maids and eunuchs. All of them, decorated with golden and azure canopies, embroidered banners, pearl curtains and embroidered fans covering from both sides, were led by sarong.

All households were filled with people, officials and the common folks alike. All paper horse shops were making paper pavilions on the street. Everywhere looked like a market. People tended to get together under blossoming trees or in the gardens, setting out wine cups and dishes, urging one another to drink and exchanged toasts. Those singers and dancers in the capital filled the pavilions and won't return until dusk. People would carry a variety of things such as (Jie) Zitui Flying Swallow, steamed cakes, long-handled knives, expensive flowers, exotic fruits, stage properties, duck eggs, as well as chickling, which was called menwaitu, literally outside local ceremony. The top of sedan chairs were decorated with willow branches and varied flowers, and curtains on the four sides. For three days since then, people all went out of the city to visit tombs, culminating on the 105th day after the winter solstice. In the market during the festival a lot of things were available such as candies, wheat cakes, cheese and milk cakes. People would come back home very late. Either when some people entered the capital gate leisurely, the light of the

绣扇双遮，纱笼前导。

士庶阗塞诸门，纸马铺皆于当街用纸衮叠成楼阁之状。四野如市，往往就芳树之下，或园圃之间，罗列杯盘，互相劝酬。都城之歌儿舞女，遍满园亭，抵暮而归。各携枣𩜶、炊饼、黄胖、掉刀，名花异果，山亭戏具，鸭卵鸡雏，谓之"门外土"。轿子即以杨柳杂花装簇顶上，四垂遮映。自此三日，皆出城上坟，但一百五日最盛。节日坊市卖稠饧、麦糕、乳酪、乳饼之类。缓入都门，斜阳御柳；醉归院落，明月梨花。诸军禁卫，各成队伍，跨马作乐四出，谓之"摔脚"。其旗旄鲜明，军容雄壮，人马精锐，又别为一景也。

第三章 风俗

　　明代的官民士庶也有阖家老小在清明节期间去郊外踏青的习俗，有时还会举行蹴鞠、走解、弹射、放风筝、荡秋千、射柳、斗草、斗鸡、斗鹌鹑等娱乐活动。踏青本来属于上巳节的内容，但是明代的上巳节已经并入清明，而扫墓又要远至郊外，所以踏青活动在明代民间十分流行。福建民谣说："踏青草，大家好呢，年年像青草。"

　　明代北京的官民士庶清明踏青都要到高梁桥游览。袁宏道《瓶花斋集》记曰："高梁桥在西直门外，京师最胜地也。两水夹堤，垂杨十余里，流急而清，鱼之沉水

setting sun suffused weeping willows, or when some were back at their own yards, dead drunk, the bright moon shone on the peach blossoms. All imperial guards in their own procession, rode horses outside for fun, which was called Shuai Jiao. They had distinguished banners and flags, majestic discipline, appearance and bearing as well as picked forces, which was indeed another spectacular scene.

During the Ming Dynasty, it was customary for the entire family, old and young, to go out to the suburbs for an outing during the Qingming Festival. Sometimes some entertainment activities such as ball playing, horseback performing, shooting, kite flying, swinging, willow shooting, grass fighting, chicken fighting as well as quail fighting. Treading on the greenery was originally characteristic of the Shangsi Festival. However, since the Shangsi Festival during the Ming Dynasty had been incorporated into the Qingming Festival and people had to go out as far as the outskirts to sweep graves, therefore hiking was very popular among the people during the Ming Dynasty, just as a folk song in Fujian Province goes, "Treading on the green grass is nice. (By doing this) Everyone is growing every year just like green grass."

During the Ming Dynasty, the Beijing people would go for an outing on the Gaoliang Bridge during the Qingming Festival, as recorded in *Pinghua Zhai Ji* by Yuan Hongdao (1568—1610), "The Gaoliang Bridge, located outside of Xizhimen Gate, is the most beautiful place. The embankment is sandwiched between two waters. Weeping willows stretch for 10-

Chapter Three
Customs

odd miles. The current is swift and clear. The scales and fins of the fishes in deep water can be clearly seen. Spreading all over the place, the red buildings and pearl pagodas set one another off among the green trees very charmingly. The colors of those small tables and mats in Western Hills were changed constantly to entertain visitors. In the height of spring, young men and women in the city gathered there, and literati and officials would also be there unless they were extremely busy." Liu Dong and Yu Yizheng during the Ming Dynasty also recorded in Volume 5 entitled *Gaoliang Bridge* in *Dijing Jingwu Lue*, "During the Qingming every year, peach trees are blooming, willow trees are budding, and green grass are growing everywhere on the bank. The capital people went sight-seeing on the Gaoliang Bridge. Some people in sedan chairs would draw the curtains open, some on horseback would gallop very fast, some spurred an ass on and some walked on foot. All of them carried

底者，鳞鬣皆见。精蓝棋置，丹楼珠塔，窈窕绿树中。而西山之在几席者，朝夕设色以娱游人。当春盛时，城中仕女云集，缙绅士大夫非甚不暇，未有不一至其地者也。"刘侗、于奕正《帝景景物略》卷五《高梁桥》也有载曰："岁清明，桃柳当候，岸草遍矣。都人踏青高梁桥，舆者则塞，骑者则驰，蹇驱徒步，既有挈携，至则棚席幕青，毡地藉草，骄妓勤优，和剧争巧"，有"扒竿、斤斗、到喇、筒子、马弹、解数、烟火、水蟾"等杂耍表演，"是日游人以万

第三章 风俗

计，簇地三四里"。

something with them. They either set up tents or put blankets on the grass to enjoy the performances of those arrogant prostitutes and hardworking actors who competed against one another". There were various shows such as "rod climbing, somersault, horseback shooting, martial skills, fireworks and so on". "On that day, there were tens of thousands of visitors covering three or four miles."

踏青并不仅仅只是郊游，还有一些娱乐身心的活动也同时举行。江南古城扬州的清明踏青活动，也有走马放鹰、斗鸡蹴鞠、劈阮弹筝、浪子相扑、童稚纸鸢和瞽者说书

Ta Qing, or treading on the greenery, was not just an outing, there were some activities entertaining for both body and spirit going on at the same time. For example, the Ta Qing activities during the Qingming Festival in Yangzhou, the age-old city in Jiangnan (south of the yangtze River) included horse race, hawk flying, cock fighting, ball playing, Zheng

Chapter Three
Customs

playing, prodigal Sumo, children flying kites and the blind's storytelling as well. Women in the capital city would play on a swing during the Qingming Festival, just as described in this *Qingming Poem*, "Everybody says outings are good in late spring, when peach and plum trees are blooming. On the bank of Qushui River are magnificent sedans, on the misty wildness trot steeds. Alas, today is rainy and windy, orioles are chirping, flowers are blossoming—another year again. Whose young beauty will return late? They are playing on colorful-roped swing". Swinging was a custom of the ancient Qingming Festival. People tied colorful ribbons to tree twigs used as the frame and made a swing which both women and children liked very much.

On Qingming, a game called She Liu (shoot willow) would be held in the palace as recorded in *Shi Xiao Lu* by Xu Shu during the Ming Dynasty, "During the reign of Yongle Emperor (1403—1424), there was a cutting-willow game...usually on Qingming." She Liu was an archery game which goes like this—put a dove in a gourd, and then hung it high on a willow tree, the dove would fly out after the game participants succeeded in shooting the gourd. The flying height of the dove served as the tally of competitions.

Whenever Qingming came, children in Jinghua, Zhejiang Province would wear all kinds of ornaments for different purposes. For example, "Wearing willow leaves is a wish for having a good maternal uncle, wearing bean flowers can make

等娱乐活动。京师妇女在清明时节荡秋千的内容正如《清明诗》所述，"尽说游行好，春深桃李天。香车旋曲水，宝马踏荒烟。风雨偏今日，莺花又一年。谁家归去晚，彩索尚秋千"。荡秋千，是古代清明节的习俗，用树桠枝为架，再拴上彩带做成秋千，妇女儿童都很喜爱。

清明之日，宫中则要举行"射柳"之戏。徐树在《识小录》记曰："永乐中，禁中有剪柳之戏……往往会于清明。"射柳是一种射箭技巧的游戏，就是将鸽子放在葫芦里，然后高挂于柳树上，游戏参加者射中葫芦后鸽子飞出，以飞鸽飞的高度来判定胜负。

每逢清明，金华地区的儿童佩戴各种饰物，"戴柳叶是盼有好娘舅，戴豆花使人明目，戴葱头盼人聪明，戴黄杨爹娘善

第三章 风俗

良，戴香荠有好兄弟，戴艾叶能避祸害"等。

　　清明时节的活动还有蹴鞠和放风筝。鞠是一种皮球，蹴鞠，就是踢球。

　　关于蹴鞠的起源，西汉学者刘向在《别录》中写道："蹴鞠者,传言黄帝所作。"无论谁发明的，只要是春天到来，在郊外踢球就成为当时的一种娱乐活动。汉代，人们把蹴

one's eyes clear, wearing shallots can make people wise, wearing boxwood will make father and mother kind-hearted, wearing shepherd's purses can bring people good brothers, and wearing mugwort leaves can ward off evils" and so on.

There were also activities such as Cu Ju and kite-flying during the Qingming Festival. Ju is a kind of ball, Cu Ju literally means "kick ball", play football.

About the origin of Cu Ju, Liu Xiang, the Western Han Dynasty scholar in *Bie Lu* wrote: "Legend has it that Cu Ju was invented by the Yellow Emperor, a legendary Chinese sovereign and culture hero." No matter who invented Cu Ju, as long as spring came, playing ball in the countryside became a recreational activity at that time. During

Chapter Three
Customs

the Han Dynasty, Cu Ju was regarded as fitness training for military purposes. At the beginning of the Western Han Dynasty (206 B.C.—25 A.D.), a type of court called Ju Cheng was built especially as football arenas in the imperial palace in Chang'an. Cu Ju was also prevalent among aristocracy in the court. During the Song Dynasty, the Cu Ju experts revered *Qingyuan miaodao Zhenjun* as their founder. There were many rules and regulations in the Qiyun Community—the famous civic Cu Ju group such as "when entering the Jü court, the ball players must worship him"; "Before meeting their teammates, all players are supposed to pick up a joss stick to worship in front of the memorial tablet of the saint"; "The Three-Animal offerings should be prepared for worshipping the founder—*Qingyuan miaodao Zhenjun*". As for who on earth was this *Qingyuan miaodao Zhenjun*, we may leave it aside for the moment, but obviously Cu Ju was already quite

鞠之地,视为"治国习武之场"。西汉初年,长安宫苑里还修建了"鞠城"作为足球竞赛场地,蹴鞠在宫廷贵族中也普遍流行。宋代的蹴鞠家奉祀清源妙道真君为祖师,著名民间蹴鞠社团齐云社的很多规矩中规定:"鞠客初入鞠场,子弟必祭之","凡诸郡先生到来,不与众圆友见礼,先到圣前拈香拜毕",要"备三牲盘案,祭献祖师——清源妙道真君"。至于这位清源妙道真君到底是谁,姑且不论,可以看出蹴鞠在当时已经是民间比较普及的活动了。清明期间的蹴鞠活

第三章 风俗

动更是让人们锻炼身体，放松身心。

popular among the people at that time. And Cu Ju activity during the Qingming Festival made people exercise and feel even more relaxed.

放风筝，也是清明时节人们所喜爱的活动。风筝，南方称为"鹞子"、北方作"纸鸢"。《墨子·鲁问》记载："公输子（按即鲁班）削竹木以为鹊，成而飞之，三日不下。"木鹊就是风筝的鼻祖，《询刍录》云："鸢首以竹为笛，使风入竹，声如筝鸣，故名风筝。"唐代，人们经常到郊外去放风筝，"夜静弦声响碧空，宫商信任往来风。依稀似曲才堪听，又被风吹

Besides Cu Ju, kite flying was also a favorite activity during the Qingming Festival. Kite was called "yaozi" (sparrow hawk) in the South while in the North it is called "Zhi Yuan" (paper kite). *Mozi: Luwen* records, "Gongshuzi (507 B.C.—444 B.C.), also known as Lu Ban, the founder of the Chinese carpentry, made a bird from bamboo and wood strips. After the completion, he flew it and it stayed up in the air for three days". The wooden bird was a proto-kite, as said in *Xun Chu Lu* compiled by Chen Yi during the Ming Dynasty, "A kite head uses bamboo strips as a flute, wind blows into the bamboo strips which vibrate and ring in the breeze like a zheng, a stringed Chinese instrument, so the popular Chinese name for the kite has become

Chapter Three
Customs

fengzheng (wind zheng)." During the Tang Dynasty, people went out to the suburbs very often to fly kites as described in the poem entitled *Kite* by Gao Pian, "At the quiet night the string sound rings high in the azure sky. Simple tones like *Gong* and *Shang* (the first two notes of the ancient Chinese five-tone scale, corresponding to 1 and 2 respectively in numbered music notation) are played by the wind at its will. It's slightly appreciatable when the notes are blurred into a song, but they are being switched into another tone very soon."

At night, people tied colorful little lanterns to the kite or the pulling string like shining stars, called "Magic Lamps". There were still others who would cut off the thread after their kites flew into the sky, an indication that the kites took away all kinds of evils, diseases and misfortunes. The

别调中"。

晚上，人们把彩色的小灯笼绑在风筝下或拉线上，像闪烁的明星，被称为"神灯"。还有人把风筝放上天空后剪断线，表示风筝带走邪魔病痛，这

第三章 风俗

样能除病消灾。这种民俗被称为"放断鹞",顾禄的《清嘉录》谓:"春之风自下而上,纸鸢因之而起,故有'清明放断鹞'之谚。"如今,许多人已不谙"放断鹞",但清明放风筝的民俗仍沿袭。

above-mentioned folk custom is called "flying a broken kite". Gu Lu in his *Qing Jia Lu*, or *Records of the Jiaqing Era of Qing Dynasty* says, "Spring wind blows bottom-up, paper kites fly upwards accordingly, so a saying goes 'fly a broken kite during the Qingming Festival'." Today, many people have no idea about what the saying means, but the folk custom of kite-flying during Qingming still remains to date.

3 饮 食
Food

Because the Qingming Festival, Hanshi Festival and Shangsi Festival have been integrated into one, the dietary customs of the Hanshi Festival are still preserved to date, but different regions differ in their eating habits during the Qingming Festival. In Shandong Province, during the Qingming Festival, people will eat eggs and cold steamed buns. In places such as Laiyang, Zhaoyuan and Changdao, people will eat eggs and cold sorghum rice, which is said to avoid hails by doing so. People in Tai'an will eat cold pancakes with raw bitter herbs wrapped in in order to have bright eyes. Around the Huangshan Mountain in Anhui Province, each year people will make wormwood cakes to eat on lunar March 3rd. A popular local saying goes, "On March 3rd, eat Artemisia cakes; eating Artemisia cakes can avoid snakes."Speaking of this custom, it has something to do with Li Shizhen (1518—1593), the renowned

由于清明节与寒食节、上巳节合为一体的关系，寒食节的饮食习俗还得以保留下来，但是各地清明的饮食习惯不尽相同。在山东，人们在清明期间吃鸡蛋和凉馒头，莱阳、招远、长岛的人吃鸡蛋和冷高粱米饭，据说不这样的话就会遭冰雹。泰安的人们吃冷煎饼卷生苦菜，据说吃了眼睛明亮。安徽黄山周围的群众，每年都制作蒿子粑粑在三月三的时候食用，当地流传了一句俗语，"三月三，吃蒿粑；吃了蒿粑避蛇害"。说起这个风俗，还

第三章 风 俗

与明代名医李时珍有关：

传说明代名医李时珍，那年他在家乡湖北蕲州，写那流传千古的《蕲蛇传》初稿时，四方向人打听各种各样的蛇，并购买各种各样的蛇去做标本。有一天，他在蕲州集上购蛇，遇见了一位刚从安徽黄山来的人。那人对他说："郎中，你要见识见识蛇吗？你得到徽州的黄山去一趟。"

"为啥？"

"那里的蛇又多又毒，毒到咬人人就死，那边人说：'土公土公，咬着不得到中；赤板赤板，咬着不得到晚。'又说：'五步龙回咬一口，棺材抬到大门口。'"

李时珍听了，点点头，说："嗯，你的话是有道理！"

那人得到夸奖，话更多了，又说："郎中，你要看蕲蛇，最好亲自到黄山脚下的祁门县去。那个县原来不叫祁门，'祁'与'蕲'谐音，因为怕人们读蕲色变，过门不入，

herbalist and acupuncturist during the Ming Dynasty:

Legend has it that when writing the first draft of his eternal *Qishe Zhuan* or *Stories of Qizhou Snakes* in his hometown—Qizhou, Qichun County, Hubei Province, Li Shizhen inquired about various snakes everywhere and purchased a variety of snakes as specimen. One day, when buying snakes in the market in Qizhou, he met a man who has just come back from the Huangshan Mountain. That man said to him: "Doctor, if you want to see real snakes, you need to go to Huangshan Mountains in Huizhou."

"Why?"

"Because there are so many and so poisonous snakes there that people will die at snake bite. Local people say that 'If Tu Gong (a kind of Pallas pit viper) bites you, you will die by noon; and if Chi Ban (another kind of Pallas pit viper) bites you, you will die by evening', and that 'If a five-pace pit viper turns and bites you, the coffin are carried to your front door'."

Hearing this, Li Shizhen nodded and said: "Well, your words make a lot of sense!"

Getting praised, that man became even more talkative, he went on, "Doctor, if you want to see Qi snakes, you'd better go to Qimen County at the foot of Huangshan Mountains in person. That county originally was not called Qimen, since the two characters are homophonic, for fear that people are too scared to go to the county when reading the

Chapter Three
Customs

character Qi as in Qi snake, a homophonic character Qi was used, hence the current name of the county Qimen."

Hearing this, Li Shizhen was on top of the world! He was then writing *QiShe Zhuan*, could it be possible that he had no interest in that topic since he was focused on the study of snakes? He thanked that man and came back home. Packing a little bit, he disguised himself as a wandering doctor and headed directly for Anhui Province.

So Li Shizhen came to Qimen. After inquiring, he knew that there was at the foot of Huangshan Mountains a village called "Single Pit". Since it has more snakes than anywhere else, people called it "Snake Pit" instead of "Single Pit". So Li Shizhen rushed directly there.

After settling down at Snake Pit, Li Shizhen lived together and had dealings with those mountain tenders, farmers, woodcutters and herb collectors every day. So not only was he familiar with the shape of the Qi snake, but he even knew clearly that it has a white body dotted with white flower patterns and two to four oblique box patterns under its flanks, and that how the snake catchers move when catching snakes and how to deal with them and make medicine after catching them. Also he confirmed that Tu Gong, Chi Ban and five-step pit viper are the most poisonous among snakes. What was even more surprising was that the Snake Pit villagers were all well. As a result, the preventive medicine he brought with him was useless. What

才改字不改音，叫作'祁门'了。"

李时珍听了，别说有多高兴了。他当时正写着《蕲蛇传》，一心研究着蛇，能不感兴趣吗?他向那人谢了，回去后，收拾了一下，就扮作游方郎中，直奔安徽。

李时珍来到祁门，经打听，知道黄山脚下有个村子，叫"单坑"，因为那里的蛇最多，所以后来人们不叫它"单坑"，而称之为"蛇坑"了。李时珍就直接赶去单坑。

李时珍在蛇坑下榻后，天天和养山的、种地的、砍柴的、采药的来来往往，生活在一起，不但熟悉蕲蛇的形状，连它是黑质白花，胁下有二至四个斜方块子花纹，以及捕蛇人的动作，捕到后怎么处理、制药，全部弄得一清二楚，也证实了土公、赤板、五步龙是蛇中剧毒。更叫他奇怪的是住在蛇坑却平安无事，以至于他带去的防备药一点也派不上用场。这是怎么一回

第三章 风 俗

事呢？

　　李时珍通过实际观察、访查，就发现村子的周围长了不少艾蒿和七叶一枝花等一些植物。这些植物发出一股气味，毒蛇根本不敢靠近。

　　这一发现使李时珍欢喜异常。他想："卤水点豆腐，一物降一物。"他就对捕蛇的人说，让他们带着艾蒿和七叶一枝花去捕蛇更安全些。捕蛇人试了试，果然蛇一闻到这些植物的气味，掉头就跑，很容易被捕蛇人从后面逮住尾巴提起来，捕蛇人再也不担心蛇咬了。

　　李时珍是个爱动脑子的人，他想要是艾蒿、七叶一枝花能食用，对防毒蛇就更好了。于是他先尝了尝这几种植物，证实它们没有毒，便采摘了一些七叶一枝花、艾蒿，洗净、磨碎，拌上糯米粉，以糖和豆沙作馅，做成粑粑，放在锅上蒸熟。人吃了这种蒿子粑粑身上就有一种香气，毒蛇嗅到这种气味就远远躲开了。乡亲们大喜，便照着李时珍那

was it?

Through actual observation and investigation, Li Shizhen found that around the village grew some plants such as mugwort and parispolyphyllasm which emit a certain smell to repel poisonous snakes.

This discovery made Li Shizhen extremely excited. He thought, "Everything has its conqueror". So he told those snake catchers that it would be safer to bring mugwort and parispolyphyllasm with them when catching snakes. The snake catchers tried, as it turned out, as soon as snakes smelled the odor of these plants, they turned and ran away, which made it easier for the catchers to lift them up by the tail from behind.

Therefore, the snake catchers didn't worry about snake bites any longer. Li Shizhen was very good at thinking. He thought, "It would be even better to prevent poisonous snakes if mugwort and parispolyphyllasm are eatable." So he first tasted these plants and confirmed that they are not toxic. Then he picked some polyphylla and mugwort, washed, ground, and mixed them with glutinous rice flour using sugar and red bean paste as fillings and made cakes. And then he steamed the raw cake in the pot. After eating this kind of cake, they emitted a kind of aroma which could drive away poisonous snakes. The folks were overjoyed, they made mugwort cakes as Li Shizhen did and ate them

Chapter Three
Customs

before working in the field and would never worry themselves about snake bite.

Li Shizhen lived in Single Pit for a while, collected plenty of snake specimens, and cured such diseases as arthritis, convulsions using dried Qi snakes.

When Li Shizhen left, the villagers around "Snake Pit" already learnt how to make mugwort cakes. In memory of this famous doctor, they would eat mugwort cakes on March 3rd every year and also use them to block snake holes. It was because after March 3rd, hibernated snakes will wake up and want to get out. They will die in the holes after eating the mugwort cakes. In the course of time, eating mugwort cakes on March 3rd became a custom.

Starting from the Tang Dynasty, the status of the Cold Food Festival gradually declined, only the seasonal food custom remained among the people. Wen Tingyun (812—870) in *Hanshi Jieri Ji Chuwang* says, "(Hanshi) falls on the 105th day (after the winter solstice)." And Yuan Zhen (779—831) in *Lian Lügong Ci* says, "Right after Hanshi, there is no fire in inns and households and the palace trees are all wearing green." Shen Quanqi in *Lingbiao Feng Hanshi* says, "I spent Hanshi outside of the Mountains, there was no sugar when spring came. Luoyang happened to be in the new *Jia Zi* Year (The Year of *Jia Zi* is the beginning of the sexagenary cycle. The next *Jia Zi* Year will come

样做蒿子粑粑，吃了后上山下田做活，就不用担心被蛇咬了。

李时珍在单坑住了一阵，采集了许多蛇的标本，用烘干的蕲蛇治疗风痹、惊搐、癫痫等症。

李时珍走后，蛇坑周围村庄的群众都已经会做蒿子粑粑。他们为了纪念这一代名医，在每年三月初三，都吃蒿子粑粑，还用蒿子粑粑堵蛇洞。因为三月三以后，经过冬眠的蛇普遍苏醒出洞，吃了蒿子粑粑便会被药死在洞中。久而久之，三月三吃蒿子粑粑便成为风俗了。

唐代以降，寒食的地位日趋式微，仅有节令食俗一项传承于民间。温庭筠《寒食节日寄楚望》云："时当一百五。"元稹《连昌宫词》云："初过寒食，店舍无烟宫树绿。"沈佺期《岭表逢寒食》云："岭外逢寒食，春来不见饧。洛阳新甲子，明日是清明。"顾禄《清嘉录》云："市上卖青帚捆坛熟藕，为居人清明祀先之品……今俗用青

第三章 风俗

糊红藕，町冷食，犹循禁火遗风，然与鬼神享饪之义不合，故仍复有烧筍烹鱼以享者。"

江浙地区在清代时要制作"青糊"或"青糍"作为清明节的冷食。这种冷食的制作方法是以南烛枝叶捣汁浸米，蒸出的饭呈青色。时下的制作方法有所改进，将青艾用石灰腌制后洗净捣碎，与米粉一起蒸成青团子。有些时候还在里面加入馅，诸如豆沙之类的。

相传，古代大禹治水，历尽千难万险为民谋福利，三过家门而不入。大禹死后，人们为了纪念他，纷纷到他坟上去上供，许多精美的供品都是大家亲手给他做的。当时，有位年轻后生提出，

60 years later), what day will be Qingming?" Gu Lu, the Qing Dynasty scholar, says in *Qingjia Lu*, "In the market, jars of cooked lotus roots bundled up with green silk strips were on sale, which were the precious sacrificial offerings the locals used for worshipping their ancestors during the Qingming Festival...Today, it is customary to make cold foods like green paste and red lotus roots, which complied with the no-fire custom handed down from the past. However, this practice is against the idea that ghosts and spirits enjoy cooked animals alive, which is why people will still burn basket traps (for fish) to cook fish for the sacrificial ceremony."

In Jiangsu and Zhejiang Provinces during the Qing Dynasty "green paste" or "green mashed rice" would be made as the cold food during the Qingming Festival. To make this kind of food, squeeze Lyonia branches and leaves into juice, immerse rice into it, the steamed rice looks blue. Nowadays the production method gets improved—use lime to marinate mugwort first, mash it after washing, then mix it with rice flour, steam, and the mugwort rice balls will be ready. Sometimes stuffings like red bean paste will be put inside.

Legend has it that when Great Yu controlled the water, he went through myriad of hardships and hazards for the well-being of the people. During years of flooding, he passed by his own house three times, but each time he did not go inside. After Great Yu died, to commemorate him, people went to his grave one after another to offer sacrifices to him and many refined offerings were made by the people

Chapter Three
Customs

with their own hands. At that time, a young man said, "Great Yu had been industrious and thrifty. He spent all his life benefiting people, so we shall let him close his eyes in the nether world. Today we presented so many fine offerings to him, would it be against his will? Could he rest in peace? We should also tell him that last year we had a big rice harvest and this year the wheat seedlings are growing very gratifyingly to make him rest assured." People thought his remarks made a lot of sense but they could not figure out what should replace those delicate offerings.

It was still that young man who came up with a good idea, "Why not use our own crops—glutinous rice and wheat leaves to make some balls and present them on the altar? This way we may tell Great Yu that last year we had a rice harvest and this year's harvest will be even better so that he will wear a smile on his face in the nether world." Everybody nodded his agreement and tried making this kind of "green rice ball". Who would have thought that the rice ball tasted bitter and astringent, not tasty at all, so they added a little lime water and stirred. They tasted again, this time, just as expected, the bitter and astringent taste disappeared, the rice ball smelled fragrant. Since then, during the Qingming Festival every year when wheat leaves turn green, people would make green rice balls and present them in front of Great Yu's tomb to show that they would never forget his meritorious service.

As time passed, this practice was handed down to date. Nowadays when the Qingming Festival

"大禹一生为民造福，勤劳节俭，我们要让他在九泉下瞑目。今天献上这么多精美的供品，岂不违背了他生前的心意?大禹能安息吗?我们还要告诉他，去年稻子丰收；今年麦苗长势喜人，让他也好放心。"人们听了这些话，觉得蛮有道理，但又想不出用什么东西来代替那些精美的供品。

后来还是这个年轻后生想出了个办法，说："我们何不用自己种的庄稼——糯米和麦叶做成团子上供?让大禹知道去年稻子丰收，今年年景将会更好，这样他也就会含笑于九泉了。"大家同意了他的办法，试做了这种"青团子"。谁知一尝，又苦又涩，真不爽口，于是又加进少许石灰水搅拌；再一尝，果然消除了苦涩味，且清香扑鼻。自此以后，每年在麦叶返青的清明节，人们就做青团子送到大禹墓前，以示不忘他的功劳。

久而久之，这一习俗也就流传下来了。人

115

第三章 风 俗

们至今仍沿袭此俗，清明时节制作青团子，带去扫墓祭祖，以表达对亲人的哀悼之情。

came every year, people would make green balls and bring them to the ancestral tombs to express their condolences to their deceased beloved.

上海还有的人家在清明节熬制桃花粥，用柳条把祭祀用过的蒸糕饼团穿起来晾干，立夏时，油煎了给小孩吃，保证不得痄夏病。浙江湖州，清明节家家裹粽子，因为俗话说"清明粽子稳牢牢"。此外，清明的时候吃螺蛳，因为"清明螺，赛只鹅"，杭州地区的百姓在清明节喜欢吃螺蛳，把

In Shanghai, some families will make peach flower porridge or string the steamed pastry used in the sacrificial ceremony with wickers and dry them during the Qingming Festival. At the beginning of summer, people will fry the dried steamed pastry and feed little kids, which will guarantee that they won't catch the Summer Fever disease. In Huzhou, Zhejiang Province, during the Qingming Festival, every family will make *zongzi*—a pyramid-shaped dumpling made of glutinous rice wrapped in bamboo or reed leaves, because a saying goes, "Qingming *zongzi* will make you stay healthy". In addition,

Chapter Three
Customs

people will eat snails during the Qingming Festival because "Qingming snails are better than geese". In Hangzhou during Qingming, people like to eat snails and put the shells on the tile to ward off evils. In Tongxiang, Zhejiang Province, a saying goes "Qingming is as big as Chinese New Year", which means people attach great importance to the family reunion dinner. In Wenzhou, however, it is customary to eat Miancai (a certain kind of vegetable) cake. Miancai is also called Qushu grass which is available only during the Qingming Festival.

螺蛳壳放在房瓦上，也具有辟邪作用。浙江桐乡有"清明大似年"的说法，重视全家团圆吃晚餐。温州一带有吃绵菜饼的习俗，绵菜即曲鼠草，是在清明时节才会有的。

In southern Shanxi Province, people will use white flour to make big steamed buns to celebrate the Qingming Festival. This kind of steamed buns, called Zi Fu, literally "son blessing", meaning that sons and grandsons have plenty of blessings, have walnuts, dates and beans inside. When visiting the grave site, people will dedicate the Zi Fu to the ancestral spirits and distribute Zi Fu among the whole family after tomb sweeping. In addition,

山西南部地区的人们用白面蒸大馍来度过清明，这种大馍中夹有核桃、红枣、豆子之类，称为"子福"，取意子孙多福。上坟时，将子福献给祖灵，扫墓完毕后全家分食。此外，黑豆凉粉也是大家所喜爱的清明食

第三章 风俗

物。北部地区也用黑豆芽和玉米面包一起食用。晋西北地区讲究用黍米磨面作饼，俗称"摊黄儿"。吕梁地区在清明后一天，要接女邀婿，俗称"清新火"。

black bean starch noodles are also people's favorite food during the Qingming Festival. People in the northern areas also eat corn bread together with black bean sprouts. In the northwest of Shanxi Province, people will grind millet into flour and make round flat cakes, commonly known as "Tan-huang-er", literally "spread out yellow (millet flour)". In Lüliang area, on the day right after the Qingming Festival, daughters and their husbands will be invited back home, commonly known as "Qing(ming) new fire".

安徽徽州地区，人们在清明节期间制作"竹叶粿"，用糯米、蒿菜和萱叶在一起浸泡半天至一天，然后再磨成粉，制作成粿。传说，吃竹叶粿与

In Huizhou, Anhui Province, people will make Zhuye Ke (bamboo leave rice cakes) during the Qingming Festival. Soak glutinous rice, mugwort and day-lily leaves together into water for half a day to one day, grind them into powder and make cakes. It is said that to eat Zhuye Ke has something to do

Chapter Three
Customs

with Zhu Yuanzhang (1328—1398), the founder and first emperor of the Ming Dynasty. The story goes as below:

They say that the very reason why Zhu Yuanzhang, Taizu of Ming, literally "Great Ancestor of Ming", was able to obtain China was that he visited incognito Zhu Sheng, a scholar in Huixi for his advice when his troops marched on Huizhou. Zhu Sheng suggested three strategies—build high walls, store sufficient grains and postpone to be throned. Overjoyed, Zhu Yuanzhang immediately asked him to be his military adviser to mastermind for his conquering the world." Zhu Sheng said smilingly, "Commander-in-chief, you already have large groups of wise counselors and capable generals and do not need sluggish country bumpkins like me. As long as you follow the three stratagems, you can reunite China in no time."Zhu Yuanzhang implored repeatedly but Zhu Sheng declined resolutely. So Zhu Yuanzhang had to leave Huixi.

Later, Zhu Yuanzhang followed the three stratagems strictly, and just as expected, he conquered China very smoothly and became the emperor. After Zhu Yuanzhang became the emperor, he went personally to Huizhou to thank Zhu Sheng and intended to ask him to enjoy the peaceful world with him in the capital city. Who would have thought that, Zhu Sheng, strange as he was, left a note and went into the mountains as a hermit. Zhu Yuanzhang failed to find the very person but get the note instead. The note read, "Your Majesty, Huizhou has few cultivated land and very large population,

明朝皇帝朱元璋有关：

明朝太祖朱元璋之所以能取得天下，是他在进兵徽州时微服私访了回溪的读书人朱升，问计于他，朱升给他献了三计：高筑墙、广积粮、缓称王。朱元璋听了大喜，当即请他当军师为他打天下出谋划策。朱升笑笑说："大帅，你手下谋士强将如云，已无须我这山野懒散之人了，只要你按这三计去做，不日就可以统一天下了。"

之后，朱元璋按"三计"办理，果然顺顺当当取得天下，当了皇帝。朱元璋当了皇帝之后，就御驾亲往徽州感谢朱升，并请朱升到京城共享太平。哪知，朱升这老夫子就是怪，悄悄留了张纸条走向深山。朱元璋找不到人，却找到纸条。条子上写的是：徽州地脊人多，是三山二水一分田，要求皇上

第三章 风俗

照顾点,减免赋税。朱元璋当即批复:"徽州免贡,务使朱升乡里世世沾皇恩!"

朱元璋临走时,带走了朱升的儿子——朱同。朱同受其父的严格教育,文武全才,加上父荫的关系,受到朱元璋的宠爱,很快登上了礼部侍郎的高位。明惠帝朱允炆即位后,更加赏识朱同,任命他为全国主考官,把选拔人才的重任交给他。朱同耿直无私,任人唯贤,政声更昭。

不久,燕王朱棣以清君侧为名,从北京起兵,攻下南京,惠帝逃走。朱棣自称明成祖,改号永乐,要"铁头御史"方孝孺为他草诏天下,方孝孺拒绝,一家二百口被弃于市。明成祖又对朱同说:

put it another way, three mountains, two waters and one-fen (small unit of land) cultivated field. Please take good care of Huizhou by reducing or remitting taxation." Zhu Yuanzhang immediately gave an official, written reply, "Huizhou is exempted from tribute (from now on). Ensure that Zhu Sheng's hometown will be bathed in the imperial grace for generations to come!"

Zhu Yuanzhang took Zhu Tong, Zhu Sheng's son, with him when he left. Strictly educated by his father, Zhu Tong was adept with both pen and sword, added to which was his social connections his father established. Very naturally, Zhu Yuanzhang bestowed great favor on Zhu Tong who therefore very quickly ascended to the high position of Libu Shilang, literally "Attendant Esquire of the Department of Ceremonial". After ascending to the throne, Zhu Yunwen, Emperor Huidi of the Ming Dynasty thought even highly of Zhu Tong and appointed him as the examiner-in-chief for the national imperial examinations in charge of selecting qualified personnel. Upright and selfless, Zhu Tong appointed people on their merits and therefore enjoyed an even better political reputation.

Soon, Zhu Di, Prince of Yan at that time, dispatched troops from Beijing under the pretext of eliminating the wicked next to the emperor, captured Nanjing and Emperor Huidi fled. Zhu Di called himself Chengzu of the Ming Dynasty (1403—1424), changed the era name into Yongle ("Perpetual Happiness"). He demanded Fang Xiaoru, known as Iron-headed Censor, to write him an inaugural

Chapter Three
Customs

address, but Fang refused. As a punishment, in addition to his own execution, the blood relations from his nine-agnate family hierarchy totaling about 200 people were killed. Zhu Di also said to Zhu Tong, "My dear minister, you see, those who submit will prosper while those who resist shall perish. So please go ahead with the address!"

Who would have thought that Zhu Tong was also stiff-necked. He said coldly, "You will earn yourself eternal infamy of usurping the throne, I won't write for you no matter what!"

Hearing this, the Yongle Emperor turned livid with rage. He would grab Zhu Tong up and crush him into pieces if he could. However, it occurred to him that after Fang Xiaoru was executed, the courtiers are still so stubborn; if he keeps killing like this, it will never end, so he held back his fury with great effort, saying, "If bamboo can produce new leaves as fruit, you can live without eating rice, I'll spare your life." Then he had Zhu Tong sent to the court-administered prison and dismissed his courtiers.

The news spread to Huizhou and became a subject of widespread comment. People were shocked and inquired about everywhere to see how to enable Zhu Tong to continue to live. They tried to figure out what Zhu Di's remarks—"if bamboo can yield new leaves as fruit" really meant. Huizhou people are smart. "One person may not in his/her mind have any strategies, but three people can

"爱卿，你可看到了，顺我者昌，逆我者亡，就请你动一下笔吧！"

哪知朱同也是个"硬头三"，他听了后冷冷地说："你难逃篡逆的千古骂名，我不会写那样的文字！"

明成祖听了，气得脸如猪肝，恨不得把朱同抓起来捏个粉碎，但是他想到方孝孺被杀，群臣仍是这样犟颈犟腔的，这样杀下去，何时是了，便强忍心头怒火，说："倘若竹能为薪叶成果，你不吃米饭，也能活下去，朕就免你一死！"之后，他就命人把朱同关进天牢，退朝了。

消息传到徽州，徽州的老乡们震惊了，议论纷纷，四下里打听有什么办法能让朱同活下去。他们在明成祖说的"竹能为薪叶成果"这句话上大做文章。徽州人是聪明的，他们"一人肚里没有计，三

第三章 风俗

人上台唱出戏",终于想出了,用蒿叶、萱叶浸泡糯米,磨成粉,做成果,其颜色与竹叶无二样,起名叫"竹叶粿"。老乡们便带着它堂而皇之进南京。

朱同知道,明成祖的这句话分明是要把他活活饿死。数天来,他都在瞅机会,准备一了百了,无奈看守看得过紧。这天上午,看守松懈了一下,朱同便以头触阶而死。

等徽州人把竹叶粿送进天牢,朱同已在早上死了。朱同死的这天,正好是清明节。徽州人为了纪念乡贤名臣——朱同父子,自此以后,每逢清明节就做竹叶粿、吃竹叶粿。久而久之,也就形成了一种乡风民俗。

四川成都地区,清明节时则以炒米做成饭团,点上各种颜色,称作"欢喜团"。有些地方清明时节有吃润饼菜的食俗,以面粉为原料烘成薄皮,俗称"润饼"或"擦饼",

perform an opera on the stage." Finally, they came up with a good idea. Soak glutinous rice, mugwort and day-lily leaves together into water, grind them into powder and then make cakes which has the same color as that of bamboo leaves and therefore was called Zhuye Ke. So they brought the cakes to Nanjing in a big way.

Zhu Tong knew very well that Zhu Di's above-mentioned sentence intended to starve him alive. For the past few days, he has been waiting for the opportunity to commit suicide in order to end all his troubles once and for all. Unfortunately the guards were alert all the time. This morning, the keepers were slightly slack, of which Zhu Tong took advantage to bump his head against the stairs and died.

When the Huizhou people sent Zhuye Ke into the imperial prison, Zhou Tong was already dead in the morning. The day when Zhu Tong died happened to be the Qingming Festival. In memory of Zhu Tong and his father who are their worthy fellow-townsmen and also meritorious officials, it has become a custom for the locals to make and eat Zhuye Ke as time passed.

In Chengdu, Sichuan Province, during the Qingming Festival rice balls will be made out of parched rice dotted with a variety of colors, called "happy rice ball". In some places during the Qingming Festival, it is customary to eat Run Bing Cai, a kind of spring roll. First roast flour into thin-skinned cake, commonly known as Run Bing or

Chapter Three
Customs

Ca Bing. When eating, spread out a flat cake, put carrot shreds, shreds of meat and coriander in it, and wrap it. Sanzi was one of the Hanshi Festival foods in ancient China. Delicate and crispy, it is still the favorite food of people today. Sanzi in different places differ greatly. There are a variety of Sanzi in ethnic minority areas. In many places after the completion of the sacrificial ceremony, people will share the ritual food.

In addition, it is customary to present painted eggs as a gift in some places. The Sui Dynasty Du Taiqing recorded in *Yuzhu Baodian* that people would dye duck eggs blue mixed with red, engrave designs on them, and give them to friends and relatives when they meet as a gift during the Hanshi and Qingming Festivals.

People in Fengtian Village, Datian County, Fujian Province, would make a plate of rice cakes that look like chicken eggs when sweeping the

第三章 风　俗

鸡蛋的米粿，当地人称之为"猴蛋粿"。猴蛋粿的来历，还是一个关于人与动物和谐相处的故事：

ancestral tombs during the Qingming Festival. Local people call it "monkey egg cake". About the origin of the "monkey egg cake", there is a folktale of man and animal living in harmony as below:

据传，丰田村朱氏的祖先是一位名叫阿十的逃荒者。他来到这里就在猴洞坡盖一个草棚安身，以养鸭为业。说也怪，他养的母鸭总是生双蛋，给他挣了不少钱，生活就渐渐好了起来。

有一年，他请来木匠，准备盖新房，这事被当地乡绅知道了，怕风水会被这个外地人夺走，就发动族人出来阻挡，锯毁他准备盖房的木料。阿十见此情景，自感前无亲、

According to the legend, the ancestor of the Zhu family in Fengtian village was called A Shi who fled from famine. After he got there, he built a thatched shed on the slope of the monkey cave and made a living by raising ducks. Strange enough, his female duck laid double eggs, he therefore earned a lot of money and his life started to get better and better.

One year, he hired a carpenter and prepared to build a new house. Unfortunately, a local gentry heard about this. For fear that this alien would take away the good Feng-shui, the gentry called the whole clan together to interfere by sawing up all his lumbers for building the house. Seeing this, A Shi felt very helpless. Without friends or relatives,

Chapter Three
Customs

he was unable to contend with the gentry just as the arm is no match for the thigh, he decided to go to other places. Right before A Shi's departure, a large group of monkeys jumped out from the woods, gathered in front of him crying all the time. They seemed to have great sympathy for A Shi's bitter experience. It just so happened that at this time the gentry again brought a crowd of people there. The monkeys stared at them for a while and saw that these people harbored evil intentions. In a twinkling of an eye, a big male monkey rushed around among the monkeys. All of a sudden, all the monkeys pounced together on the crowd who came to interfere. Biting and tearing, the monkeys shredded their clothes into pieces. The gang were scared away, since then, nobody dared to come here. Later, the monkeys fell trees, sawed lumbers and moved earth and stones for A Shi every day. And on the day when the vertical columns were lifted up as beams, many monkeys were very busy helping him in his house. When the beams were put in place, a very vigorous little monkey was elected as the "red drunk rooster" sitting on the ridge pole crying joyfully as if celebrating with A Shi the happy occasion of putting the beams in place. Soon A Shi moved into the new house and got married. He reclaimed wasteland, went in for farming and both his family and wealth were flourishing. After generations' multiplying, A Shi became the founding father of the Zhu family. Until today, in order to remember the kindness of the monkeys, the descendants of the Zhu family will present specially a plate of the "monkey egg cakes"

后无感，胳膊拧不过大腿，决定另走他乡。就在阿十临行之际，一大群猴子从树林里跳出来，围在阿十面前，吱吱吱地一直叫唤，十分同情阿十的遭遇。恰巧这时乡绅又带着一群人来了，看到这群人不怀好意，只见一只大公猴在众猴中东奔西跑，呼的一声，带领众猴一齐扑向前来干涉的人群，连咬带撕，把他们的衣裤撕成碎片，这群人被吓跑了。从此以后，再也没有人敢到这地方来了。后来，众猴天天都为阿十砍树、拉锯、搬土石。到竖柱升梁那天，许多猴子十分活跃地在房地里忙碌着。在升梁时，众猴推选出一只神采奕奕的小猴，坐在栋梁上代替"鸡踏梁"，吱吱吱地叫唤，好像和阿十共庆升梁之喜。不久，阿十搬进了新居，娶了老婆，开荒种植，家财两旺。经过世代繁衍，阿十成为朱氏门庭的开基祖，直到今天，朱氏后代为了纪念猴子的恩情，在一年一度清明祭扫祖坟时，特意供上

第三章 风俗

一盘用粳米做成的猴蛋粿做祭品。

中国的满族、赫哲族、壮族、鄂伦春族、侗族、土家族、苗族、瑶族、黎族、水族、京族、羌族等二十四个少数民族也过清明节，虽然习俗不一，但受到汉族文化的影响，扫墓祭祖、踏青郊游是基本主题。畲族在清明节期间要制作乌稔饭来分给大家，而乌稔饭的来历更是与畲族的历史有关：

唐总章二年，畲族英雄雷万兴率领畲军抗击官兵，被围困山中。时值严冬粮断，畲军只得采摘乌稔果充饥。雷万兴遂于农历三月初三日率众下山，冲出重围。从这以后，每到"三月三"，雷万兴总要召集兵将设宴庆贺那次突围胜利。并命畲军士兵采回乌稔叶，让军厨制成乌稔饭，让全军上下饱食一顿，以志纪念。这乌稔饭的制作方法并不繁杂，将采摘下来的乌稔树叶洗净，放入清水中煮沸，捞掉树叶，然后，将糯米浸泡在乌稔汤中，浸泡9

made out of glutinous rice in front of the ancestral tomb as sacrifice during the annual Qingming Festival.

China's 24 ethnic minorities including Manchu, Hezhe, Zhuang, Elunchun, Dong, Tujia, Miao, Yao, Li, Shui, Jing and Qiang also celebrate the Qingming Festival. Their customs vary, but influenced by the Han culture, tomb sweeping and springtime outing are the basic themes. The She people will make "Wu Ren Fan" (Oriental Blueberry rice) during the Qingming Festival to share with everyone. And the origin of "Wu Ren Fan" has even more to do with the history of the She minority group:

In the second year of the Zongzhang era (668—670) during the early reign (626—633) of Emperor Taizong of Tang (626—649), the She army led by Lei Wanxing, the She national hero, fought the government troops and were besieged in the mountains. It was severe winter and all food ran out. The She army had to allay their hunger with Oriental Blueberry. On March 3rd, Lei Wanxing led the army out of the mountains by breaking through the tight encirclement. From then on, on every March 3rd, Lei Wanxing would convene his generals and soldiers together and host a banquet to celebrate that breakout victory. He also ordered his soldiers to take back Oriental Blueberry leaves and demanded the military cook to make "Oriental Blueberry rice" and allowed the whole army to eat and drink their fill to mark the anniversary. To make Oriental Blueberry

Chapter Three
Customs

rice is not complicated—wash the plucked Oriental Blueberry leaves, put them into clean water to boil, take out leaves, then soak the glutinous rice into Oriental Blueberry soup for nine hours, then steam it in the cooking container, it can be eaten when cooked. The cooked Oriental Blueberry rice does not look nice due to its jet-black appearance. However, its unique fragrance distinguishes it from general glutinous rice. To commemorate the national hero, the She people will make Oriental Blueberry rice on March 3rd every year, which became the custom of the She ethnic group as time passed.

In eastern Fujian Province, the She people and Han people have been living together in harmony through the ages. Therefore, to eat Oriental Blueberry rice during the Qingming Festival became the custom that all ethnic groups in the east of Fujian Province observe.

小时后捞出，放在蒸笼里蒸煮，熟时即可食用。做好的乌稔饭，单从外表来看，不甚美观，颜色乌黑，但米香扑鼻，与一般糯米饭相比，别有一番风味。而畲族人民为纪念民族英雄，此后每年的"三月三"都要蒸乌稔饭吃，日久相沿，就成为畲家风俗。

闽东一带畲汉杂居，人民历代友好相处，乌稔饭也成为闽东各地各民族共同拥有的清明食俗。

第三章 风俗

清明时节，家家户户碾米磨面，准备各种供品。长辈带着小辈，抬着供品到祖坟上祭奠。上海人在清明前后有吃青团的食俗，据《琐碎录》记载："蜀人遇寒食日，采阳桐叶，细冬青染饭，色青而有光。"明代《七修类稿》也说："古人寒食采杨桐叶，染饭青色以祭，资阳气也，今变而为青白团子，乃此义也。"清代《清嘉录》对青团有更明确的解释："市上卖青团熟藕，为祀先之品，皆可冷食。"

山西闻喜县生产的煮饼，外皮是白芝麻的，内馅由深栗色至浅白，纤细的蜜丝金黄透亮，令人垂涎欲滴。关于闻喜煮饼，当地流传着一个耐人寻味的故事：

传说唐穆宗李恒的宰相裴度，原籍闻喜裴

During the Qingming Festival, every family will prepare for husking rice to make a variety of offerings. Parents and their children will carry offerings to the grave site to pay homage. Shanghai people has the custom of eating Qing Tuan (green ball). According to *Suosui Lu,* or *Records of Trivialities* by Wen Ge (1006—1076), the Ming Dynasty scholar, "On Hanshi every year, people in the vicinity of Sichuan Province will pick Greenback adinandra leaves and tender Holly to dye rice. The dyed rice will look green and radiant." *Qi Xiu Lei Gao,* or *Book of Seven Categories* by Lang Ying (1487—1566), the Ming Dynasty book collector also says, "During the Hanshi Festival, ancient people would pick green-back adinandra leaves to dye rice green for the sacrificial ceremony. The dyed rice can treat *yang* deficiency and has developed into green-white balls today." And *Qingjia Lu,* or *Records of the Jiaqing Era of Qing Dynasty* by Gu Lu gives a more definite explanation of Qing Tuan, "Qing Tuan and cooked lotus roots are available in the market. They are offerings for worshipping the ancestors and edible when cold."

Shanxi Wenxi steamed cakes are really mouth-watering. They are characterized by deep maroon to light white fillings, slender golden and translucent honey shreds and white sesame coating. About Wenxi cakes, there is a thought-provoking story popular among the locals as below:

Legend has it that the ancestral home of Pei Du (765—839), the Prime Minister during the reign

Chapter Three
Customs

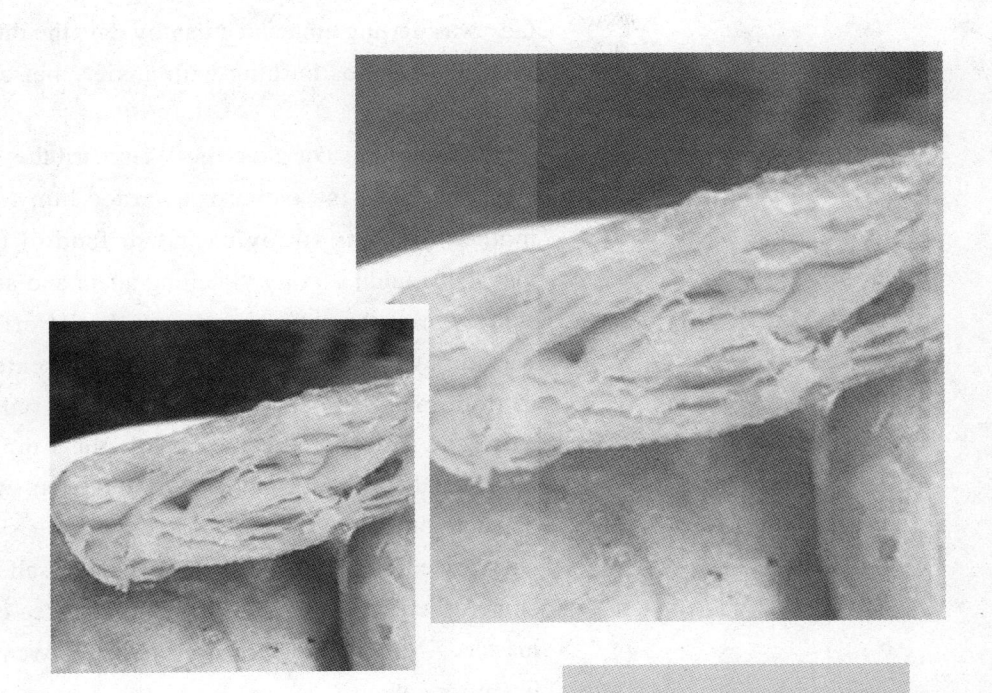

of Emperor Muzong of Tang (821—824), personal name being Li Heng, was in Peibai Village, Wenxi County. His father died when he was very young and his family was very impoverished. After he became the Prime Minister, his old mother was moved into the Prime Minister's Residence in Chang'an. Normally, moving from "thatched cottage" to "paradise", the old lady should be happy. Nobody would have expected that since arriving at the capital city, his old mother was depressed and taciturn. She often stood by the window by herself staring at the magpies on the trees in the yard, lost in thought. Filial Pei Du tried every possible means to read his mother's mind but in vain. In the course of time, the old

柏村，他自幼丧父，家境贫寒。在他成为宰相后，将其老母迁居长安宰相府。照理说，从"茅屋"进"天堂"，老人家该是欢欣。万万没想到，自抵京都后，老母整日闷闷不乐，寡言少语，时常独立窗前，眼望着院中树上的喜鹊出神。忠孝的裴度千方打听，也难以得晓老母的心事。天久日长，老人家日渐消瘦，孝子裴度心如火燎，万般无奈。

第三章 风俗

有一日，裴度将皇帝恩赐的闻喜贡品煮饼孝敬老母，老人家格外欢喜，爱不释手，闻了又闻，将已经掰开到了嘴边的煮饼又复原如初，供奉于裴父牌位前，不舍得食用。皇帝闻奏，立刻下旨：召闻喜匠师入京献艺，未曾料到来者个个露丑。无奈，皇帝又令宫中名师木之、文十、丘三一行三人前往闻喜取经。

不几日，丘三自以为学会制作煮饼，首先辞师返京献艺。他做的煮饼果真与闻喜煮饼看不出两样，皇帝大喜。但裴母吃后很不合意，说是外表样儿像，内裏馅儿硬，硌得人牙痛。但丘三仍凭着这般表面功夫也混了个八品官儿。

接着文十又急切出徒返京。文十较丘三技高一等，出自他手的煮饼，

lady was getting emaciated day by day, the dutiful son—Pei Du was burning with anxiety but could do nothing.

One day, Pei Du gave the Wenxi tribute—the steamed cakes the emperor awarded him to his mother. She was so joyful and so fond of them that she wouldn't let go. Smelling again and again, she restored the cake she already broke off and was about to put in her mouth and presented it in front of the tablet of her husband, begrudging eating it. Hearing the memorial, the Emperor immediately decreed that Wenxi cake masters would be summoned into the capital to show their skills. Unexpectedly, everyone made a fool of himself. The emperor had no choice but to send the three court masters—Mu Zhi, Wen Shi and Qiu San to Wenxi to learn from others.

A few days passed, Qiu San thought that he already knew how to make the steamed cake, so he was the first one to say bye to his master and returned to the capital to show what he had learned. The steamed cakes he made indeed looked exactly the same as the Wenxi cakes, so the emperor was overjoyed. However, Pei Du's mother was very unsatisfied after eating them. She said that they only looked like the Wenxi cakes but their fillings were so hard that her teeth ached. Still he wormed his way into the eighth-class officialdom by his superficial skills.

Then it was Wen Shi's turn to end his apprenticeship very eagerly and return to the capital. He was indeed much better than Qiu San. The steamed cakes from

Chapter Three
Customs

his hands were so good in color, fragrance, taste and shape that all officials, civilian and military alike, in the court admired them very much. This time, it was still Pei's mother who had a pretty good idea of what will happen and won't get fooled again. She put the cakes aside. Just as expected, in a few days, these cakes became too moldy and too hard to eat. Obviously, there was still a world of difference between Wen Shi's steamed cakes and Wenxi steamed ones.

But Mu Zhi was an exception. After the completion of his apprenticeship in Wenxi, Mu Zhi ran stores there and his business was brisk. He presented a memorial to Pei Du, "Wenxi steamed cake has a long history. It is easy to master its techniques but hard to get its water and soil. Without Wenxi water and soil, without Wenxi cakes. The court consumption can only depend on the annual tribute." And he refused to return to the capital with the excuse of "obtaining Wenxi soil and drawing Wenxi water". Hearing this, Pei Du flew into rage, "Isn't he digging the Feng-shui of my Pei family?" and had Mu Zhi punished thereafter. In order to avoid this huge disaster, Mu Zhi cut off his hair and became a monk at the Xiangshan Temple south of Wenxi City with "Sincerity Monk" as his religious name. He asked to be buried on the Phoenix Ridge in Wenxi after death.

In order to commemorate Sincerity Monk, people called his cake shop "Sincerity Auspicious". And the shop masters of the later generations had never been careless but constantly improving

色、香、味、形俱佳，朝中文武百官无不赞赏。还是裴母心中有数，不再上当。她将煮饼放置不食，没过几天，果真发霉变硬，不堪食用。看来，文十的煮饼与闻喜的煮饼仍有天壤之别。

唯独木之，出徒之后，就地办铺，生意兴隆。他上书裴度道："闻喜煮饼，源远流长，学工艺易，取水土难，非闻喜水土，无闻喜煮饼，宫廷享用，只赖岁岁进贡。"且以"取闻喜之土，汲闻喜之水"为由迟不归京。裴度闻后大怒道："这岂非挖吾裴家风水！"遂令治罪于木之。木之为避灭顶之灾，削发出家，在闻喜城南香山寺为僧，法名诚意和尚，并嘱死后就葬身在闻喜的凤凰岭。

人们为了纪念诚意和尚，将他开的煮饼铺起号"诚意祥"。店铺后来的师傅们为感激木之的"诚

第三章 风俗

意"，在制作煮饼时，选料考究，从不马虎，精益求精，以至于"诚意祥"成了闻喜煮饼的正宗。为了让人们像裴母一样放心食用地道的闻喜煮饼，他们还别出心裁地设计了"喜鹊登梅"包装盒，取意于裴母望鹊思乡那件事。据说，裴度后来有所醒悟，在木之死后的第一个清明节返回故乡，给父亲和木之的坟头分别添加了新土，以示生他养他的土地是祖宗留下的，只能增加，不可减少。直到今天，晋南一带还保留着清明节在祖宗坟头加土的习俗。

their skills in choosing the materials to express their sincere gratitude to Mu Zhi's sincerity. As a result, "Sincerity Auspicious" became the orthodoxy of Wenxi steamed cakes. In order to make customers like Pei Du's mother rest assured in eating the authentic Wenxi cakes, they also tried to be different from others by designing a kind of "magpies-perch-on-a-plum-tree" package cases, referring to the anecdote that Pei's mother's nostalgia when seeing magpies. It is said that Pei Du later came to realize his mistakes, more or less. So during the first Qingming Festival after Mu Zhi died, he returned to his hometown, adding new soil to the heads of both his father's and Mu Zhi's tombs to show that the land where he was born and raised was left by the ancestors and would not be reduced but only be increased instead. Until today, in southern Shanxi Province, the custom still remains that new soil is added to the ancestral grave mound during the Qingming Festival.

第四章 特色节庆地

"问西楼禁烟何处好？绿野晴天道。马穿杨柳嘶，人倚秋千笑，探莺花总教春醉倒。"明代文人王磐的《清江引·清明日出游》描绘了一幅清明出行的画卷，这动人明媚的春光和踏青，似乎几百年以来都未曾改变过。虽然历史总在改朝换代，社会总在变迁，但是传统文化的某些部分一再被继承，流传下来。

现在的清明节，固然与汉唐时期的清明佳节有一些不同，但是各地的人们仍然用自己的方式来度过清明时节，祭拜祖先、分食供品辟邪、探亲访友的聚会等，都为时下的清明节增添了几分亮丽的色彩。

Chapter Four

Distinctive Festive Places

"West Chamber, where is the best No-Fire place? At the end of the green field in the azure sky. Horses are threading their way through the weeping willows, neighing. Young beauties are swinging, giggling. Chirping birds and blooming flowers. What an intoxicating spring!"

The above poem entitled *Qingjiang Yin: Qingming-ri Chuyou* by Wang Pan (around 1470—1530), the Ming Dynasty poet, depicts a vivid picture of the outing during the Qingming Festival. For hundreds of years, it seems that the charming springtime and outings have never changed. Though history witnessed dynastic and societal changes, some part of the traditional culture has been repeatedly inherited and handed down. Though the Qingming Festival nowadays is somewhat different from that during the Han and Tang Dynasties, people in different places will still celebrate this Festival in their own way. Worshipping their ancestors, sharing offerings to ward off evils, gatherings with relatives and friends and so on have added some bright colors to the Qingming Festival today.

Chapter Four
Distinctive Festive Places

1 陕西：清明公祭
Shaanxi Province: Qingming Public Memorial

Shaanxi, as one of the important places of origin of China, has hosted so many cultural events. In recent years, the departments concerned of Shaanxi Province held the public ceremony of worshipping the Yellow Emperor during the Qingming Festival to reminisce about the merits and virtues of this initiator of Chinese civilization and express the longing of the Chinese people for this ancestor. Each year in the morning of April 5th on the Gregorian calendar, in front of the Mausoleum of the Yellow Emperor

陕西作为华夏重要起源地之一，承载了多少文化变迁。近年来，陕西省有关部门举办清明公祭轩辕黄帝典礼，以追念人文初祖功德，表达炎黄子孙的追思。每年公历4月5日上午，陕西黄帝陵前，海内外一万多名中华儿女齐聚桥山轩辕殿祭祀广场，

第四章 特色节庆地

参加典礼。

公祭典礼的流程分别是敬献花篮、宣读祭文、各族少年儿童代表齐声咏诵《振兴中华赋》和乐舞告祭仪式。告祭乐舞包括三个乐章：《赫赫始祖》《云翔大德》《龙腾盛世》，颂扬轩辕黄帝的伟大功德，表达中华儿女对先祖的崇敬之情。公祭礼毕，参加者们前去瞻仰轩辕殿，拜谒黄帝陵。

in Shaanxi Province, over 10,000 Chinese people at home and abroad will gather together at Xuanyuan Temple Worship Square on the Qiaoshan Mountain to attend the sacrificial ceremony.

The procedure of the public memorial ceremony includes presenting flower baskets, reading the funeral oration, chanting *Ode of Rejuvenating China* by the teenagers on behalf of all ethnics in unison as well as music-dance sacrificial ceremony. The sacrificial music and dance include three movements—*He He Shi Zu (Majestic Ancestor)*, *Yun Xiang Da De (Unparalleled Virtues)* and "*Long Teng Sheng Shi (Dragon Rising in a Flourishing Age)* to sing praises of the great merits and virtues of the Yellow Emperor, an expression of the reverence of the Chinese people for their ancestor. After the completion of the public memorial, the participants will pay their last respects to the Yellow Emperor Temple and the Mausoleum.

Chapter Four
Distinctive Festive Places

2 少数民族过清明
National Minorities Celebrate Qingming

China has 24 national minorities that observe the Qingming Festival such as Zhuang, Miao, She, Buyi, Bai and so on. For example, the Singing Carnival on the Third of the Third Lunar Month

中国有二十四个少数民族同胞也过清明节，例如壮族、苗族、畲族、布依族、白族

第四章　特色节庆地

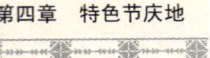

等。以壮族为例，著名节日有一年一度的"三月三"歌节，清明上坟都是隆重的庆祝方式。

清明歌会，又称为"看清明""赶清明"，是湘西苗族传统节日。除了扫墓祭祖之外，青年男女到某个地点对歌，老人们则从事贸易和会亲友。吉首市东部的苗族人民在传统的中心会场举办清明歌会，歌手们纷纷对歌、比歌、引吭高歌，热闹欢腾。

every year is a very important traditional festival for the Zhuang nationality, during which visiting the ancestral tomb is a grand way to celebrate.

Qingming Song Carnival, also called Kan (Watch) Qingming or Gan(Catch) Qingming, is a traditional festival of the Miao people in western Hunan Province. In addition to worshipping their ancestors and sweeping their tombs, the young men and women will go to a certain place to do antiphonal singing, and old people will be engaged in trade and visit friends and relatives. In eastern Jishou City, the Miao people will hold the Qingming Song Carnival in the traditional central venue,

Chapter Four
Distinctive Festive Places

during which singers would like to sing heartily in the antiphonal style or in a competitive way one after another, a sea of excitement indeed.

The Miao (Hmong) People in Western Hunan Province Spontaneously Organized Danqing Miao Song Carnival

"Cut down tree tops and bamboo shoots, I persuade you with songs and words. You'd better study or farm to better your life, for love cannot feed you all the time..." The melodious Miao songs reverberated at the Qingming riverside in Danqing Township, Jishou City, Hunan Province and brought about bursts of cheers. On the morning of April 4th, the annual Danqing Qingming Song Carnival was held here. Nearly 10,000 Miao compatriots from some counties/cities such as Jishou, Luxi, Guzhang spontaneously got together to convey their feelings and emotions through songs, floating in the air along the riverside.

Such a grand occasion has become the unique large-scale song festival of the Miao group in western Hunan Province, called Gan (catch) Qingming. According to legend, because the Miao people live scattered in the remote mountains, all daily necessities have to be bartered in from distant places. So they agreed on the day of Qingming to exchange goods while meeting with friends and relatives. Over time, it developed into today's "Miao Qingming Song Carnival".

湘西苗族群众自发举办丹青苗歌会[1]

"刀伐树尖兮伐箸伐笋，用歌劝君兮言语劝伊，君宜耕读兮衍稼富庭，情人关爱兮难尽终身……"悠扬的苗歌回荡在湘西州吉首市丹青镇的清明河畔，惹来一阵阵叫好声。4月4日上午，一年一度的丹青清明歌会在这里举行。来自吉首、泸溪、古丈等县市的近万名苗族同胞自发组织起来，以歌传情，沿河飞歌。

这样的盛况，已经成为湘西苗族特有的大型歌节——赶清明。相传，因苗族多散居在偏僻的崇山峻岭之中，一切日常用品都必须到比较远的地方赶场交换。所以，苗族人民

[1]《湘西苗族群众自发举办丹青苗歌会》，三湘统战网4月6日讯（通讯员 吉萱）http://www.hnswtzb.org/News.aspx?ArticleId=53576.

第四章　特色节庆地

便相约以清明节这一天作为自己的场期，互相交换物资，同时会见亲友。久而久之，便形成了今天的"苗族清明歌会"了。

对歌场上，苗族群众穿着民族服装，敲锣打鼓舞狮，好不热闹！苗族歌手以手托腮，引吭高歌，你唱我和，喜气洋洋。

苗族山歌没有固定字数，有时候对仗工整，有时候却不一定，取决于对歌者双方的实力和自由发挥，根据现场环境即兴表演，把看到的场景都运用在内，有时甚至是一语双关或象征比拟。通过对歌唱和，给观众带来美的享受。

In the antiphonal singing place, the Miao people dressed in national costumes perform a lion dance, playing drums and gongs. It is really lively! The Miao singers, cupping the chin in their hands, sing duets joyfully in a loud voice.

The Miao folk songs have no fixed number of words. Sometimes they have very neat matching of both sound and sense in two lines but sometimes they do not, depending on the strength and unreserved play of the antiphonal singers. According to the on-site environment, the singers perform impromptu employing all the images they saw and sometimes even some figures of speech such as puns, symbols or analogies. The singers give a treat of beauty to the audience in the way that one sings a song and the others join in the chorus.

Chapter Four
Distinctive Festive Places

3 苏北水乡：清明大会船
Waterland in Northern Jiangsu Province: Regatta

Whenever the Qingming Festival comes, China's largest water carnival—the Qingming Grand Boat Assembly will be held in Qinhu Lake in old Qintong Town located at the Subei Lixiahe River hinterland. Up to one thousand boats will attend the competition, which will attract countless audience there. This custom already has a history of over a hundred years. The anticipating ships include luxurious offering ships and ordinary artemisia ships. Before the game, each anticipating team needs to finish making their boats, testing the water and laying their boats 10 days in advance, at the same time, train those strictly-chosen punt-polers to ensure the fast speed of their boats in the game. On the contest day, people will first present potluck and pluck the willow branches to worship their ancestors and then start the game. At this time, you

每逢清明，苏北里下河腹地的溱潼古镇，都要在溱湖举行全国规模最大的水上狂欢——清明大会船，参赛会船多达千条，吸引无数观众前来观看。这一风俗已经有百余年的历史了。参赛的会船包括豪华的贡船和普通的篙船。比赛之前，各支参赛船队提前10天做好会船、试水和铺船等准备工作，同时训练精选出来的篙手，以确保比赛时行船速度快捷。会船比赛当天，人们先祭祀先人，撒出百家饭，折下柳枝后比赛开

第四章 特色节庆地

始。这时，只见湖面上插着各色彩旗的船只在拼命地往前冲，岸上的人们纷纷拍手为选手加油，最后听见急促的锣声，获得优胜的会船选手披挂红色绸带，向观众们示意。

"天下会船数溱潼，溱潼会船甲天下。"这一习俗传承了上百年，现在，溱潼清明会已列入全国十大民俗节庆活动之一、江苏省首批非物质文化遗产，国家旅游局将其列为全国四大民间传统旅游项目之一，来自美国、英国、日本、加拿大等几十个国家的驻华使节及夫人、外商及10万多中外游客，一睹"世界上最大的水上庙会"的风采。

关于会船的来历，溱潼地区有多种传说。南宋绍兴元年(1131年)，山东义民张荣、贾虎与金人转战溱潼村，大败金兵于缩头湖。义民伤亡亦甚，溱潼百姓葬阵亡将士，并于每年清明节撑篙子船，争先祭扫。久而久之，便形成撑会船的习俗。此为一说。又相传，明朝开国皇

can see a lot of boats with a variety of colored flags are trying their best to dash forward on the lake. People on the bank keep clapping their hands to cheer up the contestants. Finally the hurried sounds of gongs are heard—the winners wrapped in a red ribbon are waving to the cheering audience in acknowledgement.

"Qintong Boat Assembly is the best under heaven." The practice has lasted for more than a century. Now, Qintong Qingming Boat Assembly has been listed in China's Top 10 Folk Festivals and the first batch of Non-Material Cultural Heritage of Jiangsu Province and the Four Traditional Folk Tourism Projects by the National Tourism Bureau. The envoys from dozens of countries, including the United States, the United Kingdom, Japan, Canada, and their wives, foreign businessmen, and over 100,000 tourists at home and abroad witnessed the grandness of "the world's largest water temple".

The origin of the boat assembly: There are many legends about the origin of the boat assembly in the area of Qintong. In the first year (1131) of the Shaoxing reign period of Emperor Gaozong (1127—1162) of the Southern Song Dynasty, Zhang Rong and Jia Hu led the righteous peasants of Shandong Province to fight the Jurchen troops successively in different parts of Qintong Village and defeated them on the Suotou Lake. The righteous peasants also suffered heavy casualties. Qintong people buried the officers and men who

Chapter Four
Distinctive Festive Places

were killed in the battle and rushed out by poling a boat to sweep their tombs during the Qingming Festival every year. With the lapse of time, the custom of poling a boat came into being. This is one story. Here is another story. After Zhu Yuanzhang, the founding emperor of the Ming Dynasty ascended the throne, he was going to sweep his ancestral tomb during the Qingming Festival. Because the war lasted for a number of years, people were forced to wander about homeless. Where did his parents die, and where is his parents' grave? For the time being, he had nowhere to find and therefore was very anxious. Liu Ji, his military counselor, came up with an idea to look for his ancestral grave for him. According to the Chinese folk custom, on the day of Qingming every year, all households, big and small alike, would add new soil to their ancestral

帝朱元璋登基后，清明节要祭扫祖坟，因为打了好些年仗，百姓流离失所，他的父母死于何处，坟墓又在什么地方，一时无处找寻，心里很着急。军师刘基帮助他想出一个寻找祖坟的办法。按中国民间风俗，每年清明节这天，大家小户都要给自家的祖坟添土，烧钱化纸，表示祭祀。刘基说，过了清明，第二天派人四处查访，凡是有主坟，坟前都留下了烧钱化纸的痕迹，剩下的无主孤坟中，就不难找到皇帝先人的坟墓了。朱元璋觉得刘基的

第四章 特色节庆地

话有一定道理，就乔装打扮，坐着船在江淮一带寻找祖坟。他嫌船行得慢，下令添船加篙子，一只船上十几个人、十几根篙子，快速行进。最后，朱元璋到底有没有找到祖坟不得而知，但是朱元璋寻祖坟的诚心，感动了江淮一带的老百姓，一方传一方，一直传到泰县里下河一带。老百姓就在清明节第二天，撑船去祭孤坟，从此便演变成撑会船的习俗。还有一种传说，也是与抗倭斗争有关。明朝嘉靖年间，倭寇侵入下河神童关一带骚扰，朝廷派官兵抵抗，官兵又动员周围村庄的民众助战。于是各庄的青壮农民，纷纷组织船队前去杀敌，每条船上数十人，各执一根竹篙，行船赶路时，大家一齐撑船，到达战地，又以篙子当武器，与倭寇搏斗。由于竹篙下面的篙钻是铁制的，容易拔泥，行动不快，因此撑会船的篙子一律不带篙钻。以上传说，比见于文字记载的提前了几百年。民国时期写成的

graves and burn paper money to worship their deceased beloved. Liu Ji said that the next day after Qingming, people would be sent out everywhere for investigation. For those tombs of identified people, there must be traces of burning paper money left in front of them. So it should not be hard to find the ancestral tomb of Your Majesty among the rest of the unidentified ones. Zhu Yuanzhang thought what Liu Ji said made a lot of sense, so he disguised himself and traveled by boat along the Jiang-Huai (the Yangtze River and Huaihe River) area looking for his ancestral grave. He thought the boat trip too slow, so he ordered to increase the number of boats and poles. As a result, they had ten-odd individuals and ten-odd poles on each boat to speed up. It was unknown whether or not Zhu Yuanzhang found his ancestral tomb in the end. However, his sincerity in searching for the solitary tombs deeply touched the hearts of the masses in the Jiang-Huai area who spread the news around right down to the vicinity of the Lixia River, Tai County. So people rowed their boats to visit the solitary tombs the next day right after the Qingming Festival, which developed into the practice of the boat competition later. There is a third story also related to the battles against the Japanese pirates. During the Jiajing reign (1522—1566) of the Ming Dynasty, the Japanese pirates invaded and harassed the area of Shentong Pass along the Lixia River. The imperial government sent its officers and soldiers to resist the enemy, and the people of the surrounding villages were also mobilized to assist them in the fight. So the

Chapter Four
Distinctive Festive Places

young strong peasants in each village organized their own boat team one after another to go to the front to fight the enemies. Each boat had dozens of people on it, each one carrying a bamboo pole. When sailing, they were punting the boat together. When arriving at the battlefield, they also used their poles as weapons to fight with the Japanese pirates. Since the drill at the end of the pole is an iron head which can easily pull out mud to slow down the sailing, so no punt poles have drills on them. The legend above appeared several hundred years earlier than those found in the written records. *Gangkou Zhuzhi Ci* finished in the period of Republic of China reads, "At the beginning of the Qing Dynasty, there were many pirates around the Xia River, the people's militia were organized everywhere to help one another watching out. All of them used fast boats to report the bandit alert or exterminate the bandits. Later the bandits were annihilated, but the

《港口竹枝词》中写道："清初，下河多海匪，各处组织民团，守望相助，均以快船报告匪警或剿匪之用，迨后匪踪消灭，而团体未散，即改为东岳会戏，港口每年三月十八日举行一次，快船改名会船。"就是说，会船至迟在清朝初期就产生了。

145

第四章 特色节庆地

一、会船的种类

（一）篙船

是会船的主要道具，此船在当地叫丫梢子，长12米，宽3米，可载30名水手。他们一人一篙，篙子末尾扎块红布，水手身穿白色衬衣，青布裤子，头扎毛巾，小腿上缠着白绑布，腰围红绸子。旧时这里的篙手是随身衣服。青衣青裤，腰扎腰裙，扎个绣花的暖腰，总之，简朴、庄重、和谐。站在船头上的叫头篙，又叫站浪头，他是全船的组织者，他用篙子指挥大家的行动。篙手中有个敲锣的，叫扬锣，他随着头篙用锣声传达号令。

（二）划船

水手为女性，人手

organizations were not dismissed but changed into Dongyue Huichuan which will be held once on March 18th each year. And Kuaichuan (fast boat) was changed into Huichuan (meet boat)". That is to say, Huichuan already came into being at the beginning of the Qing Dynasty at the latest.

1. Types of Huichuan

a. Pole Boats

The main props of the boat assembly. This kind of boat is usually called Ya Shaozi, 12 meters long, 3 meters wide, with the capability of 30 sailors. Each of the sailors has one pole, to the end of which a piece of red cloth is tied. Each sailor wears a white shirt, a pair of blue cotton trousers, a towel wrapped around the head, a piece of white cloth twining round his shanks, and a piece of red silk around the waist. In old days, polers here wore everyday clothes—a blue shirt, a pair of blue pants, a waist skirt and an embroidered warm waist. In short, they look simple, dignified and harmonious. The sailor standing on the bow of the ship, called Tou Gao, literally "head pole", also known as Zhan Langtou, literally "standing (on the) waves", is the organizer of the crew and uses the pole to direct the action of everyone. There is also a poler who plays the gong to convey Tou Gao's orders.

b. Rowing Boats

The sailors are women. Each of them has a

Chapter Four
Distinctive Festive Places

paddle with a piece of red cloth round its handle. In accordance with the customs in the Qingtong area, women were not allowed to pole a Huichuan. Now dressed up in a unique way, they threw away last year's calendar—ignored the obsolete practice to participate in the boat assembly. A middle-aged woman sailor looks very fresh and cool with a white shirt, a pair of blue pants, a pink towel round the head and a piece of red silk round the waist. And girls think red beautiful. Each of them wears short hair, a red flower on the head, a red shirt, a pair of blue pants, a red belt and red leg wrappings. And the gong player looks really valiant and heroic in bearing with a red cloak on. This kind of boat only contains nine people who form a leaf floating on the surface of water—it is indeed bright and dazzling!

c. Decorated Boats

This kind of boat takes singing as its priority and does not participate in the competition. A pleasure boat consists of two boats fixed together. The top of the boat is a stage on which bands and actors, richly attired and heavily made-up, are singing and dancing. Since the 1940s, the Dang Hu Chuan, literally "sway (on the) lake boat" and dragon lamps that people originally amused themselves with also started to show their attractive bearing in the boat assembly.

d. Offering Boats

This kind of boat is used for worshiping the Buddha and the dead people. Fancy ones are characterized by a two-tier stand, upturned eaves, raised corners, four hanging lanterns, hanging

一桨，桨柄上扎着红布。按溱潼地区的风俗，以前妇女不撑会船。现在她们"翻掉老皇历"参加会船，打扮自有特色。中年妇女白衣蓝裤，头裹粉红毛巾，腰扎红绸子，清新明快。姑娘们则以红为美，剪着短头发，头插红花，服装上红下蓝，红腰带，红绑腿。扬锣的身上还披着红披风，英姿飒爽。这种船只载9个人，犹如一片树叶，飘荡在水上，耀眼夺目。

（三）花船

以演唱为主，不参加比赛。它由两条船固定在一起，上面搭着戏台，有乐队和演员，个个浓妆艳彩，且歌且舞。从20世纪40年代起，原来在岸上玩耍的荡湖船、龙灯，在会船上一展风采。

（四）供船

是供奉菩萨和祭祀亡人的船，讲究的搭两层台子，飞檐翘角，挂四只灯笼，悬挂横幅、对联，里面有僧人诵经祷告。篙手

第四章　特色节庆地

三年期满后，要以村为单位搭上一艘。新中国成立后供船的含义有了变化，只有欢送新兵入伍时才用得到它。

原来会船只有撑篙船和划船，不知什么时候，把游会的演唱和祭祀从陆上移到水上，增添了花船和供船两个花样。上世纪40年代，花船、供船传到了溱潼。

二、会船举行的时间和分布地点

溱潼会船一年一度，日期在清明日的第二天。

banners and couplets as well as monks chanting prayers inside. After the expiration of their three-year service, the polers from the same village are supposed to build one offering boat. After new China was founded, the connotation of the offering boat has changed—They are only used in giving a warm send-off to new recruits.

Originally, the boat assembly only consisted of poling boats and rowing boats, nobody knew when the concert and worship ceremony moved from land to water, and two new things, i.e. decorated boats and offering boats, appeared and both of them spread to Qintong in the 1940s.

2. Times and Venues of the Boat Assembly

Qintong Boat Assembly is held the next day after Qingming each year, to be specific, on Lunar March 18th in Gang Kou (Port) and on Lunar February

Chapter Four
Distinctive Festive Places

15th in Qiaotou (bridge head). Huichuan (fast boat) in Tai County are mainly distributed over some towns/villages including Qintong, Xingtai, Yedian, Mazhuang, Yuxi, Yuduo, Gangyang, Gangkou, Qiaotou and Shengao, in the northern waterland, an area of hundreds of square kilometers in length and width. Among them, the five villages in Qintong including Hubeikou, Huxizhuang, Hunan, Zhoucheng and Dushuzhi own the most boats. In the Gangkou area, when it comes to the number of boats, the five villages/towns, i.e. Sangjiawan, Shangxi, Dongjiatan, Sanjiaoduo and Gangkou are dominant places. And in Qiaotouxiang, boats are mainly concentrated in three villages—Huabao, Yangyuan and Libao. In general, the fast boats of all villages gather in Qintong and the scale is becoming increasingly larger.

3. The Evolution of the Boat Assembly

In the beginning, the boat assembly was held

第四章 特色节庆地

鬼神。溱潼会船特别之处是在清明第二天上孤坟，港口会船和游会水陆并行，是祭神的，桥头与庙会联系在一起，也是祭神的，它的特点是这天不去祭祖，供人娱乐。

到了20世纪40年代，会船被乡董控制，用来示威、斗殴，因而会期这天经常有殴打的事件发生，许多人被竹篙、瓦片打得头破血流，弄得不欢而散。

新中国成立后，会船得以健康发展。1950年乡亲们用会船欢送"抗美援朝，保家卫国"的青年应征入伍，表达人们对子弟兵的深情厚意。用会船欢送新兵入伍的做法，已相沿成习，一直到现在。

近几年来，会船已成了民间的一项体育活动。乡民们利用这一天来撑会船，比赛娱乐，以迎接春耕大忙的到来。

1991年会船节前，泰县人民政府正式命名溱潼

mainly to worship ghosts and spirits. What is so special about the Qintong Boat Assembly is that the next day after Qingming those solitary graves will be tended. In Gangkou, both boat and entertainment assemblies will take place by both land and water to offer sacrifices to gods. And Qiaotou boat assembly, linked with the temple fair, is also a sacrificial ritual featuring entertainment rather than ancestral worship on the very day.

In the 1940s, the boat assembly was controlled and used by the village board for demonstrations and fighting. Thus on the competition day, battering incidents took place frequently. Participants were often severely wounded by bamboo poles and tiles and ended up breaking up in discord.

After the founding of the People's Republic of China in 1949, the boat assembly developed in a orderly way. In 1950, the folks used Huichuan to give a warm send-off to the "Resist -U.S. Aggression - and -Aid - Korea (1950—1953), defend- the - homeland" young conscripts to express their profound affection to their own army. The practice of using Huichuan to see off the new recruits has been adopted as a custom until now.

In the past few years, the boat contest has become a non-government sporting activity. And the folks will take advantage of this day to enjoy themselves by poling boats for competition to greet the arrival of the busy spring ploughing.

In 1991 right before the Huichuan Festival, Tai County People's Government officially named it

Qintong Huichuan Festival and included it into the folk festivals.

4. Procedure of Qintong Huichuan Festival

Qintong is a place of strategic importance with flourishing economy and culture and interlocked rivers and streams. The water surface of Taidong River, Xiaoqinhu Lake and Jiquehu Lake are broad enough for Huichuan to flock together to distinguish themselves. The general procedure of Qintong Huichuan Festival goes as follows:

a. Boat Selection

Ten days before the Qingming Festival, flag/s will be erected by the person in charge in the village that has Huichuans. He is the administrative head of the village, responsible for the safety of Huichuans. At the upper end of a flagpole stick out green seedlings and flags. Some people think flag posts not high enough, so they just tie them to a tree. One flag pole stands for one Huichuan. The selected boats must be new and light. The shipowner whose boat/s was/were selected will be very happy.

b. Water Testing

Testing water is actually practice of movement of hands and feet. All polers are voluntary participators, the majority of whom are strong young men aged 18 and over. But old men nearing 70 years old are also welcome to participate as long as they are willing to. After registration, one needs to participate for three years in succession. If one wants to continue thereafter, it still must be three

Chapter Four
Distinctive Festive Places

会船节，将其纳入了民间艺术节的行列。

四、溱潼会船节程序

溱潼是里下河水乡重镇，经济文化发达，河汊交错，泰东河、小溱湖、鸡雀湖，水面宽阔便于会船聚汇，大显身手。

溱潼会船节大体上的程序如下：

（一）选船

清明节前10天，有会船的村子就由会头在村里竖起旗帜。他是本村的行政负责人，会船的安全由他负责。旗杆上端插着青苗和旗儿，有嫌旗杆不高的，干脆绑到树上，一条会船竖一根旗杆。选的船既要新又要轻，被选中的船主很乐意。

（二）试水

实际上是练手脚。篙手均为自愿参加，多数是18岁以上的男性青壮年，也有年届70岁的老人，只要自己愿意，报名后三年不变，如果连续，仍是三年，中途退出则认为是不吉利。旧时歧视妇

第四章 特色节庆地

女,妇女不得上会船,现在妇女能顶半边天,也和男人一样当上篙手了。男女青壮年分开组合,每天下午,篙手们就上船试水,锻炼体力,熟悉水性和"齐号"。齐号就是下篙和扬篙整齐一致,保证会船全速前进。一个人当上篙手他便会受到全家人的恭维,每天油煎鸡蛋送到他的面前,试水回来,洗脚水送到他的脚边,家务活计,全给他免掉,保证他上阵不掉队。试水的同时,舞龙灯的、摇荡湖船的和民间演唱者也抓紧排练。

(三)铺船

临近清明节,会船要洗刷干净,船舱铺上稻草,搁上跳板,保证水手站立平稳。供船、花船、荡湖船等则要美化完毕,迎接比赛。

撑会船是自发行动,费用由各人自己解囊。旧时,有个别求子心切的人自愿承担一条船的会费,

years. To quit halfway is considered to be unlucky. In old days, women were so discriminated that they were not allowed to be on board. But now women can hold up half the sky and can be sailors just like men. Male and female young adults will be separate. Every afternoon, punt-polers will go on board to test the water and have physical training to familiarize themselves with water and Qi Hao, literally "unify orders". Qi Hao refers to the same action of using the pole at the same time to ensure the movement of the boat at full speed. Once one was selected as a sailor, he/she would be given considerable preferential treatment by the whole family—Fried eggs will be put in front of him every day; when he/she comes back home after water testing, foot-washing water will be placed at his feet; and he/she is also exempted from all housework to ensure his success in the competition. While water testing is taking place, the dragon lantern performers, lake boat swayers and folk singers also intensify their rehearsals.

c. Boat Spreading

When the Qingming Festival is approaching, Huichuans must be washed clean, the cabins should be covered with straw and springboards to ensure the sailors' stable standing. The cosmetic work of offering boats, decorated boats and lake swaying boats must be finished to meet the competition.

Poling Huichuan is a spontaneous activity and each one is responsible for his/her own cost. In old times, some individuals who were eager to get a son were willing to pay for the entire boat or all the

Chapter Four
Distinctive Festive Places

poles of a boat. Those who really got a son would treat people to wine to express their gratitude.

There are three bamboo plants that provide Huichuan with poles in Jiahe of Qingtong alone. Ordinarily boatmen bought poles at different prices in line with market conditions. On the day of boat competition, any broken pole can be exchanged at the bamboo plant free of charge.

When the preparation is ready, Qingming is around the corner. During the Qingming Festival every family will sweep the ancestral grave, wrap rice dumplings and cook rice to welcome their relatives and friends to enjoy the competition and set out before daybreak the next day.

d. Leave for the Competition

This is the main part of the boat festival. Early in the morning, after the completion of the tomb sweeping, all the participating boats will sail into the stadium following the sound of the gong. At this time, market goers gradually came from all directions with shrimp cages, straw rain cape coats, capes, small shovels and sickles to barter goods, which adds more festive atmosphere. When the sun rose high, the boats gathered in the stadium. The ships would definitely fight it out when they met before but now friendly boats will set off fire crackers respectively to show their friendship to one another. On the surface of the river, the sounds of gongs, drums, pole punting and boat rowing mingled together. All kinds of red-edges-on-a-white-background flags on the stems, rectangular or triangular, decorated

或者全包船上的竹篙，真的得子者，还请酒招待，表示谢意。

为会船提供篙子的竹厂，仅溱潼夹河就有三家。平时船民买篙子随行唤价，撑会船这天，如有断篙，竹厂无偿调换。

筹备得差不多了，清明也到了。清明节家家扫墓、裹粽子、煮米饭，迎接亲友前来看会，次日天不亮出发。

（四）赴会

这是会船节的主体。凌晨，会船祭扫完毕随着锣声驶进赛区。此时，赶集的人们带着虾笼子、蓑衣、斗篷、小锹、镰刀，从四面八方陆续赶来，进行物资交流，更增添了热闹气氛。太阳升高，会船云集赛区。从前会船相遇定要比赛，分个高低，以展雄风。现在友船相见，互放爆竹，以示友谊。河面上，锣声、鼓乐声、撑篙和划船水声响成一片。船头上各式旗帜，有长方形的，也有三角形的，白

第四章 特色节庆地

底红边，上面绣着村庄的名称，旗尾和旗须装点旗帜，随风飘扬。各种类型的会船纷纷亮相，令人目不暇接。一条条篙船、划船在水手们红、白、蓝的衣服映衬下，像朵朵荷花漂浮在水上，站立整齐的水手像出征的战士，威武雄壮。花船上播放着音乐，龙灯在船上飞舞，有站着的、蹲着的、跪着的，龙身蜷成三圈，摇头摆尾，好似在戏水抢珠。荡湖船边舞边唱，千万观众翘首相望，侧耳倾听，蔚为壮观。

（五）赛船

最振奋人心的是比赛。两船对齐后，开始扬锣，"嘡！嘡！"两声，发出了竞赛的号令，接着水手们齐喊"下！下"，声音响亮，篙手两臂张开，两手挥动竹篙，笔直地两上两下，竹篙与船帮相碰发出"笃—驾"撞击声，扬篙如长矛列阵，下篙如巨蟒入水。有节奏的锣声越来越紧，船立刻从水面上腾起，犹如离弦的箭飞驰而去。

with embroidered names of the villages, the flag badges and beards, are flapping in the wind. All types of boats have appeared one after another, too many for the eyes to take in. Poling boats and rowing boats against the red, white and blue clothes look like blossoming lotus flowers floating on the water; and those neatly standing sailors look like soldiers going into battle, mighty and majestic. Music is played on the decorated boats; dragon lanterns are flying on board, some standing, some squatting and some kneeling. Its body curled into three circles, the dragon shakes its head and wags its tail just like playing in the water to grab beads. Danghu boats are singing while dancing so millions of viewers are looking up eagerly and listening attentively, which is really magnificent.

e. Boat Race

The most exciting part is race. When two ships align, gongs are beaten twice -"Tang Tang!" to issue the orders of the race. Then the sailors will cry very loudly in unison, "Go! Go!" So the polers open their arms and wave the poles with their hands, two vertical upward movements and two downward ones respectively. The clash of poles and shipboards will produce some colliding sounds, so pole raising looks like arrayed spears while to drop a pole looks like a Python slipping into the water. When the rhythmic gong sounds get heavier and heavier, the boats will jump immediately from the water surface just as an arrow leaving the bowstring is flying away.

When rowing boats, the women sailors will bend over forwards and backwards alternatively just like storm petrels skimming over the water. The heavier the gong sounds become, the faster the boats sail, which shows the fighting spirit of the people in the region of rivers and lakes. When two ships compete, to win or lose is always the final outcome. In the middle of the contest, if the winner can be determined, the gong will be beaten randomly, which means the end of the match. And repeated races will push the boat race into a climax.

After the noon, all the boats will gradually disperse. The waves in the Qinhu Lake beat against the sides of the ships of the contestants, sending out rhythmic sound like secretly telling the polers, "We are looking forward to meeting you again today next year".

5. Epilogue and Climax

The outsiders always think that the end of the boat race means the epilogue of the Huichuan Festival, but very few people know that in the epilogue there is still a joyous climax! The joyful finale is actually a trilogy consisting of the performance, wine party and giving the head pole.

a. Acting

According to the convention, before the regatta, the bigwigs of each village have long prepared for setting up the open-air theatre for the performance to thank God. Each village will hire the theatrical troupes such as Yang opera, Huai opera, Beijing

第四章　特色节庆地

请戏班子，在赛船结束的当晚开演。也有不请戏班子的，则由本庄的文娱爱好者组织起来，"乡里鼓儿乡里敲"，自娱自乐演节目。这种节目，说说唱唱，虽然简单，但泥土香味浓，乡亲们看了倍感亲切。即便在春寒料峭的夜晚，戏台前男男女女也是挤得满满的，站着看到深更半夜也不觉冷不觉倦。到了20世纪80年代，也有请电影队放电影的。但一个庄子，这天晚上要是没有演出活动，庄上人就会觉得不痛快，没有能尽兴，不如邻庄兴旺。所以，一定要唱台戏，来个

opera and acrobatics to give a show on the very night when the regatta comes to an end. There are also some villages that would rather ask their own entertainment enthusiasts to "beat their own drums" to perform to amuse themselves than hiring a theatrical troupe. This kind of talking- and- singing program, though simple, is imbued with profound local flavor, which touches the hearts of the folks. Even in the chilly early spring night, the front of the stage will be packed with men and women who will stand till midnight enjoying the show without feeling cold or tired. In the 1980s, some villages would hire a film team to show them movies. But if there is no show in a certain village on the very night, the villagers will feel upset because they haven't enjoyed themselves to the full and think their village is not as flourishing as their neighboring villages. Therefore, a performance is indispensable to usher in a prosperous future to their village.

Chapter Four
Distinctive Festive Places

b. Wine Party

On the very night when the regatta ends, the polers will, without exception, throw a heated wine party. All sailors will get together for a happy feast featuring rich homemade dishes like chicken, fish, meat and eggs rather than delicacies from land and sea on the table. The dishes are loaded with pots, wine with bowls. Everyone will drink to one's heart's content and talk of everything under heaven in a happy and unrestrained way. However, no matter how many topics they talk about, the central one will be, "Who will be awarded the Tou Gao, literally 'head pole' (a way that sailors in southeastern Zhejiang Province pole a boat using the head)?" Around this topic, everybody is eager to put in a word in the decision. At this time, their happy laughter and cheerful voices flew out of the house and made it known to their neighbors. So many friends and relatives who care about their regatta will come as if by prior agreement to add fun to the gathering by toasting them blessings one by one. Of course, each poler will follow the old practice by bringing back home a bowl of dish to share his/her happiness with the whole family and hope they are all well all year round. Some families in the neighborhood who spoil their kids and who have no poler can also come to ask for a bowl of dish for their sweeties in the hope that all will go well. And the sailors will never be stingy but try their best to meet the needs of them instead. Nobody wants to leave the table until they have drunk and eaten to

"后手翘"。

（二）酒会

赛船结束的当晚，篙手们毫无例外地要举行一场热烈的酒会。各船篙手欢聚宴饮，桌子上并不讲究山珍海味，鸡鱼肉蛋家常菜却很丰盛，菜是用盆装，酒是用碗盛，一个个开怀畅饮，相互扯起"山海经"，天上地下，无拘无束，谈的都是开心话。不过，大伙话题再多，也要转到一点上来：今年的"头篙"送给谁？围绕这个题目，七嘴八舌把头篙的得主定下来。此时，篙手们的欢声笑语，飞出屋外，惊动四邻，多少位关心他们会船赛事的亲属、朋友，将不约而同前来助兴，一一敬酒祝福。当然，篙手们也将沿袭旧例，每人端一碗饭菜回家，让全家人分享欢乐，保佑一家老少四季平安。邻里中有惯宝宝的人家，虽然没有人当篙手，也可以来讨顺遂，要一碗饭菜给家里的心肝宝贝吃。对此，篙手们也竭诚满足对方的要求，从不吝啬。大

第四章 特色节庆地

伙儿直到杯盘狼藉，酒足饭饱才肯离开桌子。至于酒会的费用，早有习俗，公吃公摊，一概由参加者负担。

（三）送头篙

也不知是什么时候形成的风俗，送头篙可以预祝人家生儿子。这对于个别久婚不孕的夫妇或新婚夫妇，颇有诱惑力，谁能够得到篙手们的青睐，成为头篙的得主，那真是一件喜事。酒会上，头篙的得主一选定，马上就会有热心人向这一家通报喜讯。这一家便立即做好迎接的准备。全家上下，满怀喜悦的心情，恭候篙手们的光临。头篙一进门，灯烛辉煌，鞭炮齐鸣，主人向篙手们奉上糖果、香茶，一一致谢。送篙者满口都是"祝贺早生贵子"的话。得主不断许诺："到时候一定请各位吃喜酒。"双方都明白，生贵子的事谁也不敢打包票，眼前只能说些祝愿的话。俗话说："没有个母鸡不生蛋，没有个女人不生养。"要是头篙的得主，这一年碰巧真生了"贵子"，

their heart's content with cups and plates strewn in disorder. And it has long been customary for all participants to share the expenses of the gathering equally.

c. Giving Head Pole

Nobody knows when the custom came into being that giving the head pole may wish the very person getting a son. This is very tempting to some couples who got married for a long time but failed to have children or newlyweds. So to find favor in the sailors' eyes and become the recipient of the head pole is indeed a happy thing. At the party, as soon as the head pole winner was selected, those warm-hearted people will immediately report the good news to his/her family who will immediately make all the necessary reception preparations. The whole family, young and old alike, are looking forward to the presence of the polers in a happy mood. No sooner have the head pole winner arrived at home than the house was brilliantly illuminated and all firecrackers were let off. The host and hostess will offer the sailors candies and tea respectively and thank them one by one. All the sailor's saying would be, "wish you getting a son soon". The winner will promise again and again, "I'll definitely invite all of you cordially to the newly-born feast of my son in the future." Both sides understand that to give birth to a son is no guarantee, all they can do is to say some "wish-" remarks for the time being. A saying goes, "There are no hens that do not lay eggs or women who cannot bear children." If the head pole

Chapter Four
Distinctive Festive Places

winner this year happened to have a boy, it would be really lively. First, the winner has to buy each sailor of the same boat a new pole, and a rich one will also treat the entire crew to food and drinks. One Huichuan has one head pole. One can imagine how many Huichuans and head poles there are in a village and how many joyful crowds of people they will affect. Folks in every village in the vicinity of Qintong have directed scene after scene of joy-seeking plays based on this or that healthy custom year after year and immersed the waterland in the joyous atmosphere.

那可就热闹了。首先要为这一船的篙手，每人添一根新篙子，富裕者还主动置办酒菜，宴请全体篙手。可以想见，一条会船有一根头篙，一个庄上，多少会船，多少头篙，牵动着多少处欢乐的人群。溱潼一带，村村舍舍的乡亲们，年复一年，以这样那样健康的风俗为"戏胆"，导演出一幕幕寻求欢乐的戏，让欢乐的气氛笼罩水乡。

后 记

清明时节，是一个祭祖追思的节日，也是亲朋好友聚会的时节。冉冉升起的轻烟中，年轻一辈在墓碑前获得了传统文化最好的传承方式——口授心传。上一代对下一代讲述祖先们的传奇故事，甜美可口的清明糕点慰藉了远方游子的思绪，欢腾热闹的歌会和传唱则让台上台下的人们一起欢呼鼓掌。

历史上的清明节，是与上巳、三月三等传统岁时节日融合在一起的。寒食节的起源，与一位忠臣的命运相关；上巳节的起源，从人们崇拜天地、乞求平安的卑微却虔诚的心愿开始；春祭与农家耕作

Postscript

Qingming is a holiday to worship and reminisce the ancestors and also a time for friends and family to get together. In the slowly rising smoke, the younger generation got the best way to inherit the traditional culture in front of the gravestone by mouth-to-mouth and mind-to-mind instruction. The older generation told the younger generation the legendary stories of the ancestors. The delicious Qingming pastries comforted the thoughts of the wanderers from afar. The jubilant and lively song carnival brought about cheering applause from people on and off the stage.

The Qingming Festival in history was mixed together with some traditional festivals such as the Shangsi Festival and Double-Third Festival. The origin of the Hanshi Festival was related to the fate of a loyal official. The origin of the Shangsi Festival started from people's worshiping heaven and earth and their humble but pious wish in begging for peace while spring offerings and farming are bound

Postscript

together with the 24 solar terms. The ancestors watched horoscope at night, trying to peep at the invisible arrangements for the destined Karma, just that nobody can see the invisible hand of fate in the Six Realms of Existence.

In fact, many Qingming-related legends reflect people's basic wish, "A harmonious family produces everything prosperous". And the wish that the country will be prosperous and the people will live in peace was also brought by the laborers who immigrated to Southeast Asia far away from home to the other end of Singapore, Malaysia, Thailand and even the Pacific Ocean. The wanderers may no longer be able to return to their motherland, but they still worship the spirits of their ancestors in foreign countries and beg for the ancestors to bless the future generations.

With the application and protection of the non-material cultural heritage, some declining festivals began revitalized. The Qingming public memorial in Shaanxi is held in a mighty way; the ethnic minorities celebrate the Qingming Festival with great gusto; and the Qingming regatta in the waterland north of Jiangsu Province pushed the Qingming celebration activities to a climax. That both the audience and the players got into the characters they were playing is exactly where the charm of the traditional culture lies in. Qingming is a season when the wanderers are easily homesick.

则与二十四节气捆绑在一起。先民们夜观星相，试图窥视冥冥之中的安排，只是六道轮回中谁也看不见那无形的命运之手。

众多与清明相关的传说故事，其实都反映了人们的小小心愿：家和万事兴。对国泰民安的企盼，也被远下南洋的劳工们带到了新加坡、马来西亚、泰国甚至太平洋的另一端。游子们可能再也不能返回祖国了，但是他们依然在异国他乡祭拜祖先的神灵，祈求先祖们保佑后人。

随着非物质文化遗产的申请与保护，一些原本式微的节日又开始焕发生机。陕西的清明公祭浩浩荡荡；少数民族的清明节，过得别有滋味；苏北水乡的清明会船比赛，则将清明的庆祝活动推向了高潮。观众们和选手们的投入，也正是传统文化传承下来的魅力所在。清明是游子们思乡的季节。

后 记

借此次编写本书的机会，我也学习到了诸多与清明节有关的文化知识。清明节，不仅是人们寄托哀思、怀念祖先的节日，也是欢聚团圆、交朋访友的日子。而年轻一代也在这种氛围和环境中将中华文明传承下去。

I have learned a lot of Qingming-related cultural knowledge during the process of writing this book. Not only is Qingming a holiday for people to give expression to their grief over the death of their loved ones and cherish the memory of the ancestors, it is also a happy time to reunite with one's family and make friends. And the younger generation will hand down the Chinese civilization in such an atmosphere and environment.

The Postscript of *Chinese Festival Culture Series*

China has developed its splendid and profound culture during its long history of 5000 years. It has a vast territory, numerous ethnic groups as well as the colorful festivals. The rich festival activities have become the invaluable tourism resources. The traditional festivals, such as the Spring Festival, the Tomb-Sweeping Day, the Dragon Boat Festival, the Mid-Autumn Day and the Double-Ninth Festival as well as the festivals of ethnic minorities, are representing the excellent traditional culture of China and have become an important carrier bearing the spirits and emotions of the Chinese people, the spirit bond of the national reunification, national unity, cultural identity and social harmony, and an inexhaustible driving force for the development of the Chinese Nation.

In order to spread the excellent traditional culture of China and build the folk festival brand for our country, the Folk Festival Commission of the China Union of Anthropological and Ethnological Science (CUAES) has worked with the Anhui People's Publishing House to publish the *Chinese*

《中国节庆文化》丛书后记

上下五千年的悠久历史孕育了灿烂辉煌的中华文化。中国地域辽阔，民族众多，节庆活动丰富多彩，而如此众多的节庆活动就是一座座珍贵丰富的旅游资源宝藏。在中华民族漫长的历史中所形成的春节、清明、端午、中秋、重阳等众多传统节日和少数民族节日，是中华民族优秀传统文化的历史积淀，是中华民族精神和情感传承的重要载体，是维系祖国统一、民族团结、文化认同、社会和谐的精神纽带，是中华民族生生不息的不竭动力。

为了传播中华民族优秀传统文化，打造中国的优秀民族节庆品牌，中国人类学民族学研究会民族节庆专业委员会与安徽人民出版社合作，在国务

《中国节庆文化》丛书后记

院新闻办公室的大力支持下，决定联合出版大型系列丛书——《中国节庆文化》丛书。为此，民族节庆专委会专门成立了《中国节庆文化》丛书编纂委员会，邀请了国际节庆协会（IFEA）主席兼首席执行官史蒂文·施迈德先生、中国文联执行副主席冯骥才先生、中国人类学民族学研究会常务副会长周明甫先生、国家民委政研室副主任兼中国人类学民族学研究会秘书长黄忠彩先生、国家民委文宣司司长武翠英女士等担任顾问，由文化部民族民间文艺发展中心主任李松担任主编，十六位知名学者组成编委会，负责丛书的组织策划、选题确定、体例拟定和作者的甄选。随后，组委会在全国范围内，遴选了五十位节庆领域知名专家学者以及有着丰富实操经验的节庆策划师共同编著。

策划《中国节庆文化》丛书，旨在弘扬中国传统文化，挖掘本土文化和独特文化，展示中华

Festival Culture Series under the support from the State Council Information Office. For this purpose, the Folk Festival Commission has established the editorial board of the *Chinese Festival Culture Series,* by inviting Mr. Steven Wood Schmader, the president and CEO of the International Festival and Events Association (IFEA); Mr. Feng Jicai, the executive vice-president of China Federation of Literary and Art Circles; Mr. Zhou Mingfu, the vice-chairman of the China Union of Anthropological and Ethnological Science (CUAES); Mr. Huang Zhongcai, the deputy director of the politics research office of the National Ethnic Affairs Commission, and the secretary-general of the China Union of Anthropological and Ethnological Science (CUAES); Ms. Wu Cuiying , the director of the Cultural Promotion Department of the National Ethnic Affairs Commission as consultants; Li Song, the director of the Folk Literature and Art Development Center of the Ministry of Culture as the chief editor; and 16 famous scholars as the members to organize, plan, select and determine the topics and determine the authors. After the establishment of the board, 50 famous experts and scholars in the field of festivals and the festival planners with extensive experiences have been invited to jointly edit the series.

The planning of the *Chinese Festival Culture Series* is to promote the traditional Chinese culture, explore the local and unique cultures, showcase the charms of the festivals of the Chinese Nation,

The Postscript of *Chinese Festival Culture Series*

express the gorgeous and colorful folk customs and create a festival image for cities. The target consumers of the series are the readers both at home and abroad who are interested in the festivals of China, and the purpose of the series is to promote the traditional culture and modern culture of China to the world and make the world know China in a better way by using the festivals as medium. The editorial board requests the editors shall integrate the theories into practice and balance the expertise and the popularity.

At present, the first part of the series will be published, namely the *Festivals in Spring*, and the editorial work of this part has been started in April, 2012 and completed in June, 2013. During this period of time, the editorial board has held six meetings to discuss with the authors and translators in terms of the compiling styles, outlines, first draft and translation to improve the draft and translation; and to consult with the publishing house in terms of the graphic design, editorial style and publishing schedule to improve the cultural quality of the series.

The first part *Festivals in Spring* is composed of 10 volumes to introduce 10 folk festivals of China from the first month to the third month of the Chinese Calendar, including the Spring Festival, the Lantern Festival, the Festival of February of the Second, the Festival of March the Third, the Tomb-Sweeping Day, the Peony Festival, the

《中国节庆文化》丛书后记

族姊妹节、彝族赛装节等，对每个节日的起源与发展、空间流布、节日习俗、海外传播、现代主要活动形式等分别进行了详细的介绍和深度的挖掘，呈现给读者的将是一幅绚丽多彩的中华节庆文化画卷。

这套丛书的出版，是民族节庆专业委员会和安徽人民出版社合作的结晶。安徽人民出版社是安徽省最早的出版社，有六十余年的建社历史，在对外传播方面走在全国出版社的前列；民族节庆专业委员会是我国节庆研究领域唯一的国家级社团，拥有丰富的专家资源和地方节庆资源。这套丛书的出版，实现了双方优势资源的整合。丛书的面世，若能对推动中国文化的对外传播，促进传统民族文化的传承与保护，展示中华民族的文化魅力，塑造节庆的品牌与形象有所裨益，我们将甚感欣慰。

掩卷沉思，《中国节庆文化》丛书凝聚着诸位作者的智慧和学养，倾注

Tibetan Calendar New Year, the Maguai Festival of the Zhuang People, the Sister Rice Festival, and the Saizhuang Festival of the Yi Ethnic Group. Each festival is introduced in detail to analyse its origin, development, distribution, customs, overseas dissemination and major activities, showing the readers a colorful picture about the Chinese festivals.

This series are the product of the cooperation between the Folk Festival Commission and the Anhui People's Publishing House. Anhui People's Publishing House is the first publishing house of its kind in Anhui Province, which has a history of more than 60 years, and has been in the leading position in terms of foreign publication. The Folk Festival Commission is the only organization at the national level in the field of the research of the Chinese festivals, which has rich expert resources and local festival resources. The series have integrated the advantageous resources of both parties. We will be delighted and gratified to see that the series could promote the foreign dissemination of the Chinese culture, promote the inheritance and preservation of the traditional and folk cultures, express the cultural charms of China and build the festival brand and image of China.

In deep meditation, the *Chinese Festival Culture Series* bears the wisdoms and knowledge of all of its authors and the great effort of the editors, and

The Postscript of *Chinese Festival Culture Series*

explains the splendid cultures of the Chinese Nation. We hereby sincerely express our gratitude to the members of the board, the authors, the translators, and the personnel in the publishing house for their great effort and to all friends from all walks of the society for their support. We hope you can provide your invaluable opinions for us to further promote the following work so as to show the world our excellent festival culture.

Editorial Board of
Chinese Festival Culture Series
December, 2013

着编纂者的心血和付出,也诠释着中华民族文化的灿烂与辉煌。在此,真诚感谢各位编委会成员、丛书作者、译者、出版社工作人员付出的辛勤劳动,以及各界朋友对丛书编纂工作的鼎力支持!希望各位读者对丛书多提宝贵意见,以便我们进一步完善后续作品,将更加璀璨的节庆文化呈现在世界面前。

《中国节庆文化》
丛书编委会
2013年12月